Royal Ladies

QUEENS REGNANT, QUEENS CONSORT, PRINCESSES OF WALES AND PRINCESSES ROYAL

Royal Ladies

QUEENS REGNANT, QUEENS CONSORT, PRINCESSES OF WALES AND PRINCESSES ROYAL

Alex Cobban MBE

ATHENA PRESS
LONDON

ROYAL LADIES
Queens Regnant, Queens Consort,
Princesses of Wales and Princesses Royal
Copyright © Alex Cobban 2008

ISBN: 978 1 84748 396 6

First published 2008 by
ATHENA PRESS
Queen's House, 2 Holly Road
Twickenham TW1 4EG
United Kingdom

Printed for Athena Press

Contents

Tables

Introduction

The history books tell us a great deal about our kings and queens who have ruled in their own right, but less is known of the queens consort. These ladies from the royal houses of Europe or from the flower of the European aristocracy have produced the children who became future kings and queens.

Who does not know about Anne Boleyn, or in fact any of Henry VIII's wives? They are well written about, as are the queens Henrietta Maria, Eleanor of Aquitaine, Alexandra or the most recent Queen Mother; but what of the others?

What of the Eleanors of Provence and Castile, the Joans of Brittany and Navarre, the Matildas of Flanders, Boulogne or Scotland, Anne of Denmark, Ann Neville or Anne Hyde, the Marys of Bohun and Modena, the Catherines de Valois or of Braganza, or Avisa of Gloucester?

In the pages of this book I hope to highlight these and the many other queens consort.

Researching the facts suggests that many of the queens consort were promised in marriage as mere children. There were reasons for these early matchings, just as there were reasons why Henry VIII tossed Catherine of Aragon aside to marry Anne Boleyn and why three years later Anne had to be executed. The reasons may not seem acceptable to us today but the reasons given at the time were acceptable, or made acceptable.

If someone had written a book and invented the story of Henry VIII and his six wives we may have considered such a work far-fetched. Yet it was all true and 'stranger than fiction'.

In the pages of this book we shall see how kings, princes, ambassadors and clergy were sent abroad to search the courts of Europe for suitable brides for one monarch. In many cases they were not searching for a love match but a means to an end. Alliances could be made between countries previously at war and often large, sometimes very large dowries accompanied the wedding agreements, so making good matches even more important.

Each queen consort is taken in chronological order and dates are given of her birth and death and where she is buried. To complete the story of our queens I have included the six queens regnant, i.e. Mary Tudor, Elizabeth I, Mary II, Anne, Victoria and Elizabeth II. A further section has been devoted to the Princesses of Wales, numbering eight, although there have been twenty-one Princes of Wales and nineteen holders of the title Welsh prince.

I hope you will find this book as interesting as I have found the research.

Alex Cobban

Historical Background

The Romans came in AD 43 after two previous expeditions by Julius Caesar in 55 and 54 BC. The Emperor Claudius wanted to add to his empire and although it was almost 100 years since the visits by Julius Caesar, Claudius decided the time was right. There was little opposition to the Roman army's arrival and they soon settled down at Colchester, St Albans and London. The Romans left in approximately AD 410 and there followed the period of the Dark Ages.

Of this period of 150–160 years little is known of our history. The first mention of the Saxons seems to be AD 494 and by 100 years later, in 597, Augustine came to convert the country to Christianity. By AD 604 Bishop Mellitus had set up a church where St Paul's now stands and by 616 King Sebert of the East Saxons had established his church on Thorney Island – now Westminster Abbey.

It was Edward the Confessor who built the abbey in stone, on the island of thorns or Thorney Island. He dearly wanted to see it completed before his death. The abbey was finally consecrated on 28 December 1065; Edward was too ill to attend and died eight days later. Harold of Wessex on the death of Edward decided to have himself crowned King on 6 January, the day of Edward the Confessor's funeral. The throne had previously been promised to William, Duke of Normandy. This not only antagonised William but also Harold Hardrada of Norway. Harold of Norway immediately invaded and Harold of Wessex met him at Stamford Bridge, south of York, where Harold of Norway lost and gave up his right to the throne. By this time William of Normandy had set sail for England and Harold of Wessex had to march his army 250 miles south to meet William at the Battle of Hastings on 14 October 1066. At this battle Harold of Wessex lost his eye, his life and his throne.

William of Normandy now became known as William the Conqueror and he chose Christmas Day in the year of 1066 to be crowned in Edward the Confessor's recently completed Westminster Abbey.

Since William the Conqueror's coronation we have had forty-one monarchs of which thirty-nine have been crowned in Westminster Abbey. Two Edwards never got to their coronations: Edward V, who was murdered in the Tower of London in 1483, and Edward VIII, who abdicated in 1936.

Matilda of Flanders

Wife of William the Conqueror
Born 1032
Died 1083
Buried Holy Trinity, Caen

Matilda and the Tapestry

William the Conqueror was born at Falaise in 1027 and became the Duke of Normandy in 1035. During a visit to his cousin Edward the Confessor in 1051 he received the promise of the succession to the throne of England. On Edward the Confessor's death in 1066 Harold of Wessex proclaimed himself King. William then set sail from Barfleur to take possession of his lands. There followed the battle of Hastings on 14 October 1066 at which Harold of Wessex was killed and William began his conquest of England. In this one year Edward the Confessor died, Harold was crowned King and later killed in battle and William was crowned King of England.

William the Conqueror's queen Matilda was the daughter of Baldwin V, Count of Flanders and his second wife, Adela, who was the daughter of Robert II of France and sister of Henry I of France. William wanted to marry Matilda in 1049 but the marriage was forbidden by the Council of Rheims because it was declared they were too closely connected by family. They were finally married in 1053. It was not until 1059 that a later council under Nicholas I granted a dispensation for marriage. As her share in the atonement required from her and her husband, Matilda built the Abbey of the Holy Trinity at Caen. While William was away on his Conquest of England she ruled Normandy in his place. Early in 1068 she made the journey to

England and on 11 May was crowned Queen, either in Westminster Abbey or Winchester Cathedral.

Matilda was considered to be handsome in appearance and noble in person. She was very rich and dispensed a great deal of her fortune to help others. She had four sons: Robert, who succeeded his father with the Duchy; Richard, who was killed hunting in the New Forest; William and Henry, who both became kings of England. There may have also been six daughters. Certainly there was Cecilia, who became a nun at the church at Caen; Constance, who married Alan of Brittany in 1086; Adeliza, who died young; Adela, who married Stephen of Blois; and Agatha, who was promised to Edwin, Earl of Mercia and betrothed to Alfonso of Spain, but married neither.

When William was preparing for his invasion of England she presented him with his own ship called the *Mora* and on the prow was a golden image of a boy with his right hand pointing towards England while in his left hand he carried an ivory horn.

Whereas the Anglo-Saxon Chronicles document that period of history in writing, the Bayeux Tapestry portrays the same period in pictures. It might be expected that this would portray only the Norman point of view. It outlines the visit of Harold of Wessex to William in 1064 and ends with the Battle of Hastings in 1066. It even shows Halley's Comet, which was visible in 1066; an astrologer is shown explaining to Harold that it could be a portent of death. The tapestry was commissioned by Bishop Odo of Bayeux (William's half-brother) and was reputedly stitched by Queen Matilda and her ladies-in-waiting.

The tapestry is actually an embroidery. It was almost certainly completed in England and it measures 76½ yards long by 20 inches deep. A curious feature seems to be that all the English are portrayed with moustaches while the French are clean-shaven.

Children	Born	Died
Robert	1052	1134
Richard	1054	1075 killed by a stag
Cecilia	1055	1126

Adeliza	1055	1061
William (II)	1056	1100 (William Rufus)
Constance	1057	1090 (possibly poisoned by her servants)
Adela	1062	1137
Agatha	1064	1074
Henry (I)	1068	1135
Matilda	?	1112

Historical Background

On his death in 1087, after a twenty-two-year rule, William the Conqueror was succeeded by his son, another William (II), who ruled from 1087–1100. He might well have ruled a lot longer, but he was killed during a hunting expedition in the New Forest on 2 August 1100. He was killed by an arrow said to have been fired by Sir William Tyrell. There were those who believed the arrow was fired by another and not an accident. The future Henry I was in the hunting party.

By 1097 William Rufus (Red Hair) had completed an extension to the Palace of Westminster by building the Westminster Hall, which William said was 'a mere bedchamber' to what he envisaged for the palace.

William II was succeeded by his brother, Henry I, who would rule for thirty-five years. His son William was lost in the wreck of the White Ship. It was perhaps the pride of seventeen-year-old Prince William, who wanted to command his own ship from Barfleur, France to England. The White Ship was laden with several of Henry's illegitimate children, earls, barons, a nephew of the German Emperor and several senior churchmen.

They set sail with a drunken crew and the ship struck a rock near the Normandy coast. All were to perish except for the ship's butcher. Prince William was King Henry I's only male heir; he had in addition approximately twenty illegitimate children.

Henry I died in December 1135 and Stephen, the King's nephew, was declared King by the citizens of London. Henry had died after a meal of lampreys. There followed nineteen long winters of Stephen's reign.

Stephen was the son of Adela, daughter of William the Conqueror. Civil war broke out because Matilda, daughter of Henry I, claimed the throne. However, by the Treaty of Wallingford it was agreed that when Stephen died he would be succeeded by Prince Henry, Matilda's son.

Matilda of Scotland

1st Wife of Henry I
Born 1080
Died 1118
Buried Westminster Abbey

Mold, the Good Queen

This particular Matilda was the daughter of Malcolm III of Scotland, and Margaret, who was granddaughter of Edmund Ironside. She was born in 1080 and her godfather was Robert, Duke of Normandy. She was baptised Edith but Matilda, Maud, Mold or Matilde were names she was known by.

She was educated at Romsey, where she was compelled to wear the nun's black veil as a protestation against the brutality of the Normans, who were then ravaging the coast. When her father, Malcolm III, came to visit her in the veil he pulled it off, saying, 'I had not intended you to be a nun but a husband for Count Alan of Richmond.' He took her back to Scotland in the year 1093. By the end of that year, Alan of Richmond, King Malcolm III and his wife Margaret were all dead.

Matilda sought refuge in England with an uncle, Edgar Atheling, and at his home she met the Earl of Warenne, who wanted her hand in marriage. She was however being reserved for a person of greater standing than an Earl – to take the hand of the king, Henry I of England. She was more than willing to marry Henry, but as in many royal marriages an objection was raised because she had worn the black veil.

Archbishop Anselum was told by Matilda that she had never taken the vows as a nun and as this proved to be true approval was finally given. In November 1100 she was both married and crowned by Archbishop Anselum in Westminster Abbey.

Her first child was born in 1101 but died. A year later followed the birth of a daughter, Matilda.

The first Austin Priory in England, at Holy Trinity, Aldgate, was founded by the Queen in 1108. It was also the first in London to be dissolved during the reign of Henry VIII. In 1532 Parliament confirmed the gift of the priory to the King because it was written that the Prior had departed from the monastery, leaving it profaned and dissolute.

Matilda had a bridge built at Bow near Stratford, East London, over the River Lea. She then passed it over to the care of the nuns of Barking. She also took an interest in the plight of lepers, washing their feet and kissing their scars and founding a hospital for them at St Giles in the Fields. St Giles is the patron saint of outcasts. It was to her also that condemned prisoners were given a cup of charity, their last drink as they passed the hospital. It was in this parish that the Great Plague began in 1665.

King Henry and Queen Matilda had a second child, named William. He grew up to manhood quickly and won his spurs fighting at the side of his father, He had faced death in battle, was popular with his soldiers but William was still only seventeen years of age. In 1120 on a return journey from France with his father he was given his own ship, 'the White Ship'. It sank near the Normandy coast and all but one were lost.

The young Prince William was drowned; some say he had tried to save one of his illegitimate sisters.

Matilda died on 1 May 1118 and was buried in Westminster Abbey believing she had left a son and daughter to ensure the line of succession.

Children	*Born*	*Died*
Matilda	1102	1167
William	1103	1120

Adeliza or Adela of Louvain

2nd wife of Henry I
Born between 1103 and 1106
Died 1151
Buried in Affligem Abbey, Belgium

Henry I married his second wife, Adela, in 1121 at Windsor, and later, she was crowned queen. She was the daughter of the warlord of Louvain, Godfrey VI, Count of Louvain.

A gentle and retiring person, she took no part in politics but did take great interest in the literature of the day. On Henry I's death in 1135 she seems to disappear from view, probably to the castle at Arundel – she was certainly residing there in 1139. Ultimately she was to marry again, to William de Albini.

She made gifts to Henry's abbey at Reading and to the cathedral at Chichester. She was buried at Reading Abbey.

Adela had seven children[1]. However, Henry I had six children by Sybilla, daughter of Sir Robert Corbet; three by Ansfrida; one by Nesta, Princess of Dehenbarth; one by Edith, daughter of the Lord of Greystoke; one by Isabella of Meulan, daughter of the Earl of Leicester; one by another Edith; and twelve by various unknown mothers. A total of twenty-five illegitimate children.

---

[1] All Adela's children were with her second husband William de Albini, 1st Earl of Arundel. She failed to produce any children in fifteen years of marriage to Henry.

Matilda of Boulogne

Wife of King Stephen
Born 1103
Died 1152
Buried Faversham Abbey

The Queen Who Founded Abbeys

Matilda of Boulogne was the only child of Eustace III, Count of Boulogne and his wife, Mary, daughter of Malcolm III, King of Scotland. The year of Matilda's birth is given as 1103. Before she was twenty-two years of age she was married to Stephen of Blois, who had been endowed with large estates in England and Normandy. Her father, Eustace, also owned estates in England and Boulogne, which came to Matilda as the only child. On 22 March 1136 Matilda was crowned Queen.

Matilda gave birth to a son, Eustace, named after her father, and he was to be invested as Duke of Normandy and promised in marriage to Constance, the sister of the French King, when Matilda's husband Stephen was captured at the battle of Lincoln in 1141.

Ranulf, Earl of Chester, was Stephen's most serious opponent and he had seized Lincoln Castle. Stephen waited until he was reasonably sure Ranulf had disbanded most of his troops. The citizens then opened their gates and Stephen entered, but Ranulf returned with a large army. Although the King put up a bold fight he was hit by a stone and captured.

Matilda, with the King's leading officer William of Ypres, began rallying the army for the King's release. Eventually a bargain was struck and for the release of Stephen she would release Robert, Earl of Gloucester, half-brother of Matilda, wife of

Henry I. Stephen's rule lasted for nineteen years and went down in history as 'the nineteen long winters when God and his saints slept'.

Matilda shared with William of Ypres the task of founding Faversham Abbey. She was also responsible for the foundation of a preceptory of Knights Templar at Cowley, Oxford. Five years later she founded the Cistercian Abbey at Coggeshall, Essex. By the Tower of London stood the hospital of St Katherine's founded by her in 1148.

Matilda had two children who died young: Baldwin and Matilda. Three children survived her: William, who became by marriage Earl of Warenne; Mary, who was brought up at the nunnery at Stratford and eventually went to Ramsey as Abbess; and Eustace, who died soon after his mother and just before his father.

Matilda at the end of April 1152 fell ill at Hedington Castle, Essex where she died on 3 May. At her request she was buried at Faversham Abbey to be joined there by her husband Stephen when he died in 1154.

Children	Born	Died
Eustace	1130	1153
Baldwin	?	before 1135
Marie	1136	1182
William	1137	1159
Matilda	?	?

Historical Background: The Plantagenets

Henry II succeeded to the throne on the death of King Stephen; this began the new line of kings. The Angevin Kings are so called from their decent from Geoffrey of Anjou.

It was during Henry II's reign that Thomas Becket was murdered in his Cathedral at Canterbury on 29 December 1170. He was made a saint three years later.

After Henry II had deserted his wife for his mistress Rosamund Clifford, his wife, Queen Eleanor, set the children against their father. Henry's was a turbulent reign. When Henry heard that his favourite son, John, had taken arms against him he said, 'Enough, now let things go as they may. I care no more for myself or the world.' He died two days later on 6 July 1189.

Richard I assumed the throne as the eldest son. Although he was King for more than ten years he spent most of his time abroad at the Crusades.

Richard having no heir, the throne went to his brother John in 1199. Within six years he was embroiled with Pope Innocent III about the choice of a new archbishop of Canterbury. The outcome of this was that the barons forced John to Runnymede on 18 June 1215 to seal the Magna Carta because they felt that John had mortgaged the country to the Pope and agreed to certain damnation laid down by Rome. King John died the following year and his nine-year-old son Henry succeeded as Henry III. A regency was formed with William, Earl of Pembroke as the Earl Marshal of England until the King reached the age of maturity.

During Henry III's reign, in 1265 the first House of Commons was formed by Simon de Montfort. Also during this reign, most of the Dominican (Blackfriars) and Franciscan (Greyfriars) came.

Eleanor of Aquitaine

Wife of Henry II
Born 1122
Died 1204
Buried Fontrevault Abbey

The Rich and Beautiful Eleanor

When Henry II assumed the throne at the age of twenty-one he was already married to Eleanor of Aquitaine, the divorced wife of Louis VII of France. Queen Eleanor had been given Tower Royal, situated where Cannon Street meets Queen Street in the City of London, and she also had a place in Bermondsey.

Eleanor was probably considered the richest, most talked about and loveliest woman of the age. Aquitaine, which was the dowry that came to Henry on his marriage to Eleanor, consisted of the rich meadows and vineyards of Poiton, Lusignan, Angoumois, Saintonge and Periford, and the areas of Limousin and Auvergne were also included. Henry realised his marriage to Eleanor would make him ruler of lands twice as extensive as those of Louis of France.

Henry married Eleanor on 18 May 1152 at Bordeaux Cathedral, Gascony.

Henry brought his new bride and queen to England where she was watched with some curiosity; the circumstances of her divorce were, to some, a shocking affair. Just two years after her arrival in England, her coronation took place in Westminster Abbey. Earlier that year she had given birth to a son named William, but he died quite young. The second child, another son, was born and named Henry, followed by a daughter, Matilda, who would eventually marry the Duke of Saxony. Richard was the next born – Richard Coeur de Lion as he came to be – who married Berengaria of Navarre. Geoffrey came next, who married the Countess of Brittany. Their sixth child was named after her mother; she married the King of Castile. Another daughter, named Joanna, followed; she eventually married William II of Sicily. The last child, a son, was named John.

King Henry II, despite having eight children, was said to be having a secret love affair with Rosamund Clifford, whom we are told was kept hidden away in a secret bower in the maze at Woodstock Palace. The bower was so well hidden that the only way to find it was to follow a silken thread through the maze, which only Henry knew about. One version of this romantic love story was that Henry came out of the bower one day and the thread had caught on his spur and was noticed by Eleanor. Using the thread the queen discovered the whereabouts of the secret love nest. Eleanor is then said to have gone to the bower with a goblet of poison in one hand and a dagger in the other and Rosamund, 'Fair Rosamund', was given the choice of which way she wanted to die. She, who was regarded as the loveliest creature in the world, chose the poison. How much of this story is actually true is difficult to assess. There certainly was a 'Fair Rosamund', and she probably was the King's mistress, but when the love affair was discovered, Rosamund is said to have gone into the convent at Godstow.

Henry II died in 1189 and it was his wish to be buried in Fontrevault Abbey.

Their son Richard was now King Richard I. This man of great stature spent most of his reign out of the country. Of almost eleven years as king, he spent only six months in England. Eleanor returned to England from France to bring up her youngest child, John. She was also instrumental in securing the release of Richard from captivity in Austria.

The Dowager Queen Eleanor was now getting old. She had been queen for sixty-seven years and was now eighty-two years old, an extremely great age for this period of history. She still had her own teeth and was quite slim. When she passed away in the year 1204 she was buried at her own request at Fontrevault Abbey between her husband Henry II, and her son, Richard I, who died in 1199.

Children	Born	Died	Buried
William	1153	1156	Wallingford Castle, Bucks
Henry	1155	1183	Le Mans Cathedral
Matilda	1156	1189	Brunswick Cathedral
Richard	1157	1199	Fontrevault Abbey
Geoffre	1158	1186	Notre Dame (trodden to death by his horse during a tournament)
Eleanor	1162	1214	Abbey of Las Huelgas
Joan	1165	1199	Fontrevault Abbey
John	1166	1216	Worcester Cathedral

Berengaria of Navarre

Wife of Richard the Lionheart

Born 1172

Died 1230

Buried L'Epau Abbey

The Queen Who Never Saw England

Berengaria was the wife chosen by King Richard I himself, who professed he wanted no second-hand goods. He met her through her brother, Sancho the Strong. Richard and Sancho had much in common including their love of arms, horses, dogs, music and battle. It seems Berengaria was of small build and dark and she had a love of poetry and music.

When Richard became King of England he could choose his own bride and it had to be Berengaria. His mother, Eleanor of Aquitaine, left for Navarre to bring back his bride. She had longed for the day when Richard would send for her and she was more than agreeable to marrying him. He was a chivalrous knight, a king of England and the Angevin Empire.

The couple were to marry in Cyprus at the Chapel of St George, Limassol on 12 May 1191, he wearing a rose-coloured tunic of satin and a mantle of striped silver covered with half moons, and with a scarlet bonnet on his head. It seems that whatever the bride wore was not considered important enough to record for history. The wedding feast lasted three days.

The honeymoon was short, for Richard had to leave to take part in the siege of Acre and to fight Saladin's army. The French army also arrived; the besieging had been going on for two years; and Saladin arrived with a bigger army until it was not certain who was the besieged and who was the besieger. Eventually

Richard and the various armies in support of the Holy Church took Acre.

Berengaria and Joanna (Richard's sister) were ensconced in great comfort in one of the marble palaces of the city. After the third crusade and more success for Richard a peace was arranged with Saladin for a period of three years, three months, three weeks, three days, three hours, three minutes and three seconds. This meant that, for the time being at least, Acre and Jaffe remained in the hands of the Christians.

Richard decided to leave Palestine and decreed that Berengaria should too but in a separate ship. This, he said, was safer. That was Richard's excuse but it was becoming clear that the marriage was not the perfect match that they had hoped for. She had seen little of Richard during the past four years. Although this was due to the Crusades, the marriage was certainly cooling off, and Richard seemed to prefer male company. Berengaria had been a good and faithful wife, obedient, loving, and the fault of the break-up seemed to rest with Richard.

As instructed, Berengaria and her sister-in-law, Joanne, set sail and eventually arrived at Messina, then going overland to Rome. In Rome they were shocked to find that the balric belonging to Richard made of blue velvet and with the 'R' insignia in gold thread was being offered for sale. The King, they were told, had disappeared!

It has been said that after a long search it was Blondel the court musician who was sent to find his master. At every castle he sang his song beneath the walls, a song that he and Richard had composed together in alternate verses. If he found Richard he would respond to the song. He was eventually rewarded for his long trek. It was then agreed that a ransom be paid for the release of the King. On receiving his freedom he left for Antwerp, where a ship would take him to England.

Once back in England he relieved his brother John of his powers. This he did at his mother's insistence, to absolve John of his treachery. However, as if to reassure himself and his people of his return to his kingdom he decided to have a second coronation. Here was an ideal moment to have Berengaria crowned Queen. This would be one way of bringing them together again. But it was not to be; she was not invited to cross from France for the ceremony.

Richard decided to build a great castle, the Château Gaillard, and the work took a year. Soon after its completion Richard became ill and, being reminded by one of his priests attending him that he had not treated his consort fairly, he sent for Berengaria to join him. When his health had sufficiently recovered he decided they should spend Christmas together at Aquitaine. This was a happy time for him, perhaps the happiest they had experienced. Shortly after Christmas Richard was off again, this time to fight Philip of France, but now he took Berengaria with him.

During a skirmish Richard was wounded by an arrow fired by one of his own men – a boy named Pierre or Peter Basile, also known as Bertran de Gurdun, among other names, who was the archer of a mercenary captain named Mercadier. The wound unfortunately became gangrenous and Richard died. Although the King had forgiven the boy, he was arrested, flayed alive and hanged.

Berengaria was there to tend Richard's wound and care for him but it was not long before his strength ebbed away and the King died in 1199. He had been king for nearly eleven years but had spent most of his time away from the kingdom.

Berengaria lived for another thirty years at Mons and there founded the abbey of L'Epau. She died in 1230 in the abbey, this poor neglected queen, so loyal, so faithful to her husband, who had travelled long journeys during his campaigns and nursed him when he was ill. She was different from all the other queen consorts because she was never to see the country of which she was queen.

Children: None

Avisa of Gloucester

1st Wife of King John
Born 1176 (or possibly before)
Died 1217
Buried Canterbury Cathedral

Avisa of Gloucester was sometimes called Isabella or Hadwisa or Avice. At first a marriage was proposed between King John and Alice, daughter of Humbert III, Count of Maurienne and in 1172 a marriage contract was signed. This was never honoured owing to Henry II, John's father, refusing to give away any of his lands as part of a marriage dowry.

On 28 September 1186, William, Earl of Gloucester agreed to give his daughter's hand in marriage. The marriage took palace on 29 May 1189 at Marlborough, despite remonstrations from Archbishop Bladin because John was related to Avisa, three times removed.

Because Avisa produced no children, John got a divorce granted by the Bishop of Normandy-Aquitaine; Avisa was later to marry Geoffrey de Mandeville, son of the Earl of Essex.

Children: None

Isabella of Angoulême

2nd Wife of King John
Born 1188
Died 1246
Buried Fontrevault Abbey

In the small province of Angoumois with its capital city called Angoulême was the château of the Count Aymer de Taillefer. Here lived the count with his beautiful daughter, Isabella. Some said she was the most beautiful woman in the world. She was betrothed by her parents to Hugh of Lusignan, a handsome young knight.

King John decided to make a Royal progress through his western kingdom of Angevin. A stop was made at the château of the count. The count wanted to impress King John and so his daughter Isabella was to attend the ceremony. She looked extremely lovely in her gown of scarlet and gold and wearing a gold circlet on her head and a very fine veil falling about the shoulders.

King John was now aged thirty-two years and she was but fifteen years of age. The King was already married, but that did not deter him from choosing a beautiful young woman to grace his court.

John's wife, Avisa of Gloucester, was a distant relative but it was not difficult to obtain a divorce. John and Isabella were married in Bordeaux Cathedral.

When Hugh of Lusignan returned from visiting England and found his bride-to-be had married the King he immediately challenged the King to a duel. But John said he was too important to fight duels and appointed a champion. Hugh refused to fight a substitute; so began unrest in France.

The newlyweds set sail for England and she was crowned Queen in Westminster Abbey. The King appeared for his coronation with a robe covered in emeralds and rubies, even having sapphires sewn into his gloves – a glittering figure he must have been. His new wife, who loved fine clothes and would indulge herself when possible, was to receive only a small wardrobe from John and practically no jewels, despite the fact he had chests full, accumulated from various Norman Kings.

Trouble was brewing in France and John, who wanted to protect his interests, could find little support for his cause. When he arrived in Normandy, the French army had already taken many of the castles and besieged several cities. King John was accompanied by Isabella and Queen Eleanor. John's mother, now old and walking with a stick, summoned up support in France. She went to Mirabeau and took possession of the keep and held it until John arrived. The town was not expecting his arrival and was taken – and so was Hugh de Lusignon, the handsome young knight once betrothed to Isabella. Because of Queen Eleanor's interception Hugh was not executed but sent instead to imprisonment in Bristol. He was eventually released and returned to France.

It was on 12 October 1207 that Isabella, after seven years without producing a child, gave birth to Henry (Henry III). There was to follow another son, Richard, and three daughters; Joan, the eldest, was at the age of eleven married to Alexander, King of Scotland.

The Barons were rising against the King because of the King mortgaging the country to the Pope. From this upheaval with the Pope, the Church at Canterbury and the Barons came Magna Carta in 1215.

The following year found the King on the move. Having lost several wagons of treasure in the Wash (an inlet of water on the East Coast) and without funds he went to Swineshead, a Cistercian monastery, and decided to rest. He ate a hearty meal and finished it with peaches and ale. Almost immediately he was taken ill and said the monks had poisoned him. Still in acute pain he travelled on, first by horse, then by sitter to Sleaford and then to Newark and the palace of the Bishop of Lincoln. He was able to dictate a statement, the main point being the appointing of William Marshal, the only man he really trusted, as guardian of the future King, young prince Henry.

King John passed away in 1216 and at his request he was buried at Worcester. Isabella, still in her thirties and very attractive, returned to Angoulême where her daughter Joan was being brought up as a future bride for Hugh de Lusignon. When the two met again Hugh declared that he still loved her – she must marry him. They were married and the story of Isabella of Angoulême and Hugh came to a happy ending.

Children[1]	Born	Died
Henry (III)	1207	1272
Richard	1209	1272
Joan	1210	1238 (married Alexander of Scotland)
Isabella	1214	1241
Eleanor	1215	1275

---

[1] King John is said to have fathered twelve illegitimate children.

Eleanor of Provence

Wife of Henry III
Born 1220
Died 1291
Buried Amesbury

La Belle

When Henry III was searching for a bride his eyes turned towards the younger of the two Scottish princesses, Marion, despite the fact she was ten years older than himself. The council did not sanction this plan. The reason they gave was that Hugh de Burgh had married Princess Margaret of Scotland and it would be derogatory to the Royal House to have one of its subjects as a brother-in-law. He then turned his eyes to Europe and the three European courts – (a) the daughter of Leopold of Austria, (b) daughter of the Count of Brittany, (c) a Bohemian princess – but none of these came to fruition.

The small area of Provence under Raimund Berenger IV, Count of Provence, had four ladies to be considered. Marguerita, dark hair and fair complexion, was first; Eleanor 'La Belle', so nicknamed because of her beauty; Sanchia, the third, possessing the charm 'of incomplete beauty'; finally Beatrice, who was also of considerable beauty.

Eleanor, 'La Belle', was but fourteen years of age and Henry suggested to the Count that they should agree to the marriage. Since Provence was in a poor state, marriage with a king of England would be a great match. A dowry figure of 20,000 marks was set, but this came down to 3,000 marks. However, so keen was Henry to get Eleanor that he would settle with or without money being involved. Agreement was reached and the bridal party arrived at Dover on 4 January 1236.

On arrival at Canterbury they were married by the Archbishop and then travelled to London for the coronation of the Queen. They were met by the Lord Mayor, Andrew Buckerel, and a procession of over thirty people on horseback dressed in fur-trimmed cloaks and tunics of gold. It was during this very festive and colourful occasion that Henry of Avranches, a poet, was placed on the King's household as the King's Versificator – the first Poet Laureate.

The first-born, Edward, grew to be a very tall young man and was given the nickname 'Longshanks', whereas the second son, Edmund, because known as 'Crouchback', possibly because of a deformity – he was his father's favourite.

Henry III had to leave for Gascony to settle matters relating to Simon de Montfort and on his departure he appointed Eleanor as Regent. She took on the role seriously, sitting at the Court of Pleas and presiding over the Council. It was clear from the time of her arrival in London that she hated the place and the Londoners and now she had the opportunity to show them her aggressive nature. She immediately demanded all the back payments of queen's gold. It was part of the Queen's prerogative to be a paid a tenth part of all fines which came to the crown. The King had imposed fines on the weakest excuses and the City had paid rather than fall foul of the King. Eleanor was now demanding her share.

To show that she meant what she said the two Sheriffs, Richard Picard and John de Northampton, were taken prisoner and the City had no alternative but to pay the queen's gold. Since the King had left for war in Gascony she then demanded of the City funds to fight the war. Once again the City refused and this time Eleanor arrested several prominent City merchants, including the Lord Mayor, Richard Hardel.

In Gascony things were going very much in the King's favour. In agreeing a peace it was decided that Prince Edward, the King's son from Eleanor of Provence, would marry the Infanta of Castile, Eleanora. The marriage duly took place at the monastery of Las Huelgas and Eleanor of Provence left England to be at the wedding.

Later the City would get its reward. When the Queen left the Tower of London by barge the citizens lined London Bridge and waited to pelt her with stones and mud, rotten fruit and vegetables. They were also shouting, 'Down with the witch, drown the witch!'

Queen Eleanor left for France to try to find support for the Royal cause and get her husband released from captivity. She had not only pawned all the jewels but many personal possessions as well.

The King had been captured by Simon de Montfort during the battle of Lewes.

On 29 October 1265 Queen Eleanor returned to England accompanied by Dona Eleanora, the young wife of Prince Edward and now known as Eleanor.

When Eleanor died on 25 June 1291 her instructions were that she should be buried in Amesbury where she took the veil, but her heart to be buried in the Franciscan priory of Greyfriars in London.

Of Eleanor's children, Edward became Edward I. Margaret married Alexander III of Scotland, and Isabella married John de Dreux, Duke of Brittany.

Children	Born	Died
Edward (I)	1239	1309
Margaret	1240	1275
Beatrice	1242	1275
Edmund	1245	1296
Richard	1247	1256
John	1250	1256
William	1250	1256
Katherine	1252	1257
Henry		died young

Historical Background

Edward I, 'Longshanks', succeeded his father, Henry III. He was a great castle builder. Edward's aim was to consolidate his kingdom by adding Wales and Scotland to England. In Wales he succeeded in his conquest and promised them their first Prince of Wales of English descent. However, he met his match with Robert Bruce and William Wallace, the latter eventually being betrayed and brought to Smithfields in London to be hanged, drawn and quartered.

Edward died in 1307, succeeded by his son, another Edward, who was twenty-three years of age, strong and witty. His failing was his infatuation with a young French noble, Piers Gaveston, and would result in his deposition, his imprisonment in Berkeley Castle, and his horrible death in 1327.

Edward III, son of Edward II, was a warrior and he and his son, the Black Prince, made this an Age of Chivalry. The Black Prince won victories for his father at Crécy in 1346 and at Poitiers in 1356. The foundation of the Order of Chivalry, 'The Most Noble Order of the Garter', was due to Edward III and the Black Prince was one of the founding knights in 1348. Unfortunately the Black Prince died in 1376, a year before his father, thereby leaving the throne to his son Richard (II).

During Edward III's reign the Black Death raged in 1348 and one third of the population died as a result of the bubonic plague, carried by flea-infested rats, which eventually turned the body black!

Richard II was little more than a child when he became King. Within four years he was embroiled in the Peasants' Revolt of 1311, stemming from an imposition of poll tax. However, Richard II, like Edward II, was deposed and the nobles were now in revolt against the King and supporting Henry Bolingbroke – John of Gaunt's son. Richard II was confined in Pontefract in Yorkshire and probably murdered there in 1400.

Eleanor of Castile

1st wife of Edward I
Born 1244
Died 1290
Buried Westminster Abbey

Eleanor the Faithful

Prince Edward, son of Henry III and Eleanor of Provence, was a handsome young prince, tall in stature, eventually reaching a height of 6 ft 4½ in. He became known as Longshanks, and every inch of him was that of a chivalrous and brave knight. Henry was anxious that the heir to the throne should marry and an alliance with Spain seemed to be the right cause.

Alfonso the Wise of Castile had a half-sister, the infanta Dona Eleanora of Castile. She was now ten years of age and the English representatives came to make the arrangements and carry out negotiations. Dona Eleanora's mother was Joanna of Ponthieu, who had been tossed aside when Henry III was looking for a bride in order that he could marry Eleanor of Provence. It was agreed this could not and should not happen again. It was therefore laid down that Prince Edward must appear in person in Bruges not later than five weeks before Michaelmas the following year to claim his bride. If he did not appear then the marriage contract would be cancelled.

So in October of that next year the marriage of Prince Edward at the age of fifteen to the little Eleanora aged eleven took place at Las Huelgas monastery, and so began one of the true great romances of English history. Edward remained in Europe while his young bride was to spend several years in England before becoming a wife in anything but name.

A few years had passed and Princess Eleanor, now twenty years of age, had grown up into an intelligent and beautiful lady with a sweet and gracious figure. The Princess had been given Guildford as her residence and Henry had the castle specially prepared. He specified it should have glazed windows, a raised hearth, a chimney and a wardrobe. There she gave birth to her second son, named Henry.

Prince Edward was to leave for yet another Crusade, this time taking his wife with him. Separation from her now was unthinkable. When she was told it was dangerous to go on Crusades, she replied, 'The way to heaven is just as easy from the Holy Land as it is from London.'

It was 1272 when Henry III died and Prince Edward was still away at the Crusades. When he finally got the news of his father's death the funeral had already taken place in Westminster Abbey. On the same day he was told his uncle Richard of Cornwall and Edward's first-born son, John, had also died. He eventually returned to England on 2 August 1274 with Eleanor, and they were crowned together on 19 August.

The actual number of children born to Edward and Eleanor is still an arguable point. It was most likely sixteen. There were only four sons. Of the daughters there were Eleanor, Joanna, Margaret, Berengaria, Mary, Elizabeth, Alice, Blanche, Beatrice and Katherine. Of the sons Henry and John both died young and Alfonso, named after Eleanor's brother, also died before adulthood. Edward, the remaining son, was to become Edward II. Edward was born on Welsh soil at Caernarvon Castle and it is said that King Edward held his newborn child above his head and said, 'Here is what you wanted – a Prince of Wales who speaks neither English nor French and his first words shall be of the Welsh language.' How true this is is not clear but certainly he was the first Welsh Prince of Wales.

The Royal Family had chosen Windsor as their home. It was close enough to London for the King and large enough for his large family of what seemed to be delicate sons and beautiful daughters. This arrangement seemed idyllic, the happy couple watching their family grow up. They spent time together hawking and hunting and moving from palace to palace as the mood took them.

Because of trouble which had broken out in Scotland Edward decided to march north with his army. He spent a few days hunting in Sherwood Forest. The Queen remained at Harby and almost immediately she was struck by a fever. It was not considered too serious at first but the King was told. He hurried back to be at her bedside and he reached Harby just in time, for she died shortly afterwards on 28 November 1290, aged forty-seven.

The King was stricken with grief and remained completely close to his queen for two days. He wrote, 'We cannot cease to love a consort now that she is dead whom we loved so deeply when alive.'

Eleanor's coffin was filled with aromatic spices before the body was laid inside. The funeral began its journey to Westminster. Edward decided she should be remembered in some significant way and chose the idea of stone crosses, to be placed at each place where the funeral procession rested overnight. Lincoln was the first, the second at St Peters Hill near Grantham, the third at Stamford, the fourth at Geddington, the fifth was at Hardingstone, a mile from Northampton, the sixth at Stretford, the seventh at Dunstable, the eighth at St Albans, the ninth at Walthamstow, the tenth at Waltham Abbey, the eleventh at Cheapside and the twelfth at the village of Charing (now Trafalgar Square). Several of these were destroyed by Cromwell's Roundheads.

Eleanor was greatly loved by the people and the statue on her tomb in Westminster Abbey by William Torrell, done shortly after her death, shows a figure of beauty, delicate features and a gentle smile.

Wax candles burned around her tomb for 300 years, showing she had not been forgotten, this devoted wife, mother and queen.

Children	Born	Died
Daughter	1255	stillborn
Katherine	1264	1264
Joan	1265	1265
John	1266	1271

Henry	1268	1274
Eleanor	1264	1298
Daughter (probably Julianna)	1271	1271
Joan of Acre	1265	1265
Alphonso	1273	1284
Margaret	1275	after 1333
Berengaria	1276	1278
Daughter[1]	1278	1278
Mary	1279	1332
Son[2]	1280	1281
Elizabeth	1282	1316
Edward (II)	1284	1327

---

[1] Died soon after birth; no contemporary evidence of her name.
[2] Also died soon after birth; no contemporary evidence of his name.

Margaret of France (Marguerite)

2nd wife of Edward I
Born 1277
Died 1313
Buried Greyfriars, Newgate St, London

Edward waited nine years before marrying for a second time. He had set his sights on Blanche, daughter of the King of France. In return France would get Gascony, considered then to be one of the jewels in the French crown. However, it was not to be. Blanche favoured a match with Rudolph, Duke of Austria. The name of Margaret was entered into the treaty of marriage, and although it was a blow to Edward's pride that he was turned down, he agreed to marry Marguerite. The marriage took place at Canterbury on 8 September 1299. Although there was a big difference in their ages, Edward and Marguerite seemed very happy.

When Edward left for more battles in Scotland, he left his young wife in the Tower of London apartments. The following year, his queen went with him as Eleanor had done. At Cawood Castle in Yorkshire, a prince was born and named Edmund, and the next year at Woodstock another prince was born and named Thomas. There followed a daughter named Eleanor, after Edward's first wife.

The years of battle campaign were taking their toll on King Edward. He was now sixty-eight years of age and he gave his son strict orders that after his death 100 English knights were to go to the Crusades and to remain for a year, and with them was to go the King's heart. His body, he asked, should be boiled to get rid of the flesh and his bones wrapped in a hammock and carried in front of his army when fighting in Scotland, so he may be present at the time of victory in spirit, if not in body.

The king died on 7 July 1307. Marguerite was a gentle and beautiful lady who won the affections of her stepchildren and, despite the fact she was still quite young at thirty years of age, she never remarried. She spent the rest of her life building the Greyfriars Church in London and was buried there when she died in 1318.

Children	Born	Died
Thomas	1300	1338
Edmund	1301	1330
Eleanor	1306	1311

Isabella of France

Wife of Edward II
Born 1296
Died 1358
Buried Greyfriars Church, Newgate St, London (body),
*   and at Gloucester Cathedral (heart)*

The Shewolf

Edward II, son of Edward I and Eleanor of Castile, became King in 1307 and was to rule for twenty years. Isabella of France, his wife, was first known as 'Isabella the Fair' but later she was to be called 'The Shewolf'.

Arrangements were made for the wedding of Isabella to Edward to take place at the cathedral of Boulogne. Isabella was just thirteen years of age, and was fair and beautiful. The assembled gathering was, to say the least, illustrious, including Philip the Fair, the kings of Sicily, Navarre, and Romans, all with their sparkling, bejewelled queens, the Archduke of Austria, Charles of Valois, the Duke of Brabant and the dowager queen Marguerite of England, plus many princes, princesses and lords.

It must have seemed odd that the couple were seeing each other for the first time. They looked happy enough, despite the fact that Isabella had been told strange things about Edward. He thought of her as no more than a little doll-shaped girl. As the handsome couple stood at the altar, looking so happy, who would have thought the marriage was doomed for failure.

When the couple arrived in England, they were met at Dover by Piers Gaveston, looking radiant in his jewelled clothes. Against him, the King looked like a second-class citizen. The King and Piers embraced each other with more enthusiasm than that of a normal welcome. England's new Queen was given a rapturous welcome in London and the streets were decorated with flags and bunting, while the conduits ran with red wine for all to fill their cups.

The coronation was planned for 25 February and, once again, Piers Gaveston strutted about in magnificent clothes and carried Edward's crown. It seems he was in charge of all the Abbey arrangements and this had not been handled very well. One knight was trampled and died trying to find his seat. The ceremony took three hours longer than first thought and not only did the King and Queen have to put up with this inconvenience, but at the coronation banquet, food was not ready on time and when it was finally declared to be ready it was not properly cooked.

Eventually, after the queen had written to her father, Philip the Fair, he sent an emissary. He secured the assistance of the barons, who had no love for Gaveston, and it was finally agreed, despite the King's objection, that Piers should be stripped of all his offices and honours.

The bishops also wanted him banished. He was sent to Ireland and after he returned he was banished. He returned and was banished once again. Piers Gaveston was eventually to return again and this time he was arrested; a form of trial was held and he was sentenced to be executed. He was beheaded. The King was not only enraged by the treatment of his friend, but he was also grief-stricken and wept openly.

After this sad episode, the King went to Windsor to be with Isabella and soon the glad news of the birth of a son was announced. The next King of England would be Edward III, and had been born to Isabella who was eighteen years of age. She was to play the dutiful wife, despite past events, and gave birth to another son, John, followed by two daughters, Eleanor, born at Woodstock, and Joanne, who was born at the Tower of London.

The King once again turned his attentions to young men, finding company with Hugh le Despenser, but this affair was not allowed to go on for long before he was executed by being hanged, drawn and quartered.

Because of this second affair, things were beginning to turn against the King. It was known the queen had turned to Roger Mortimer, Earl of March, for support and many were demanding the removal of the King, saying the lives of Queen Isabella and Prince Edward would be endangered if he remained in power.

After several skirmishes and attempts by the King to gain the full support of Parliament and the knights, the King was finally captured and taken to the castle at Llantrisant. Eventually, he was moved to Kenilworth, which was not the splendid castle it became later. His deposition was not being demanded and Isabella was now shedding tears, perhaps to conceal her real feelings or perhaps in repentance. Prince Edward was offered the crown, but refused unless his father's consent to the deposition was first received.

King Edward said, 'Much as I grieve at having incurred the ill will of the people, I am glad they have chosen my eldest son to be King.'

Edward was moved once more to Berkeley Castle at Isabella's request. There is no actual proof that she had a direct hand in the following events, but she must have certainly known about them from Roger Mortimer. Edward was finally put to death in the castle dungeon by the cruel and callous method of red-hot pokers inserted inside the body.

Roger Mortimer's period of importance was to come quickly to an end. He was arrested and executed at Tyburn. Queen Isabella was now named 'The Shewolf' and was out of favour because of her possible involvement in the King's death. She went to Berkhampstead and then to the royal palace at Eltham. She was by now in full repentance for what had been done, whether in her name or not.

The queen finally died on 22 August 1358, aged sixty-three and having lived twenty-eight years in exile. Her last wish was that she wanted to be buried in the Greyfriars churchyard in the City of London, but her heart to be removed and buried with her husband Edward II at Gloucester Cathedral.

Children	Born	Died
Edward (III)	1312	1377
John	1316	1336
Eleanor	1318	1355
Joan	1321	1362

Philippa of Hainault

Wife of Edward III
Born 1315
Died 1369
Buried Westminster Abbey

The Queen and Alice Perrers

William V, 'The Good Count of Hainault, Holland, Zealand and Lord of Friesland' and Joan, daughter of Charles of France, had four beautiful daughters. When Edward III was looking for wife, any of the four would have been acceptable to the King. The marriage council were sent to choose one. One member of the council, Adam of Orleton, was given a secret instruction from the King: 'Use your own judgement in selecting one of the four – provided it is Philippa!'

The future queen of England was duly married to Edward at her Flemish home by proclamation. On 23 December 1327, she arrived in London to a rapturous reception. She travelled north to be with the king and they were officially married on 24 January 1328 at York Minster. The reason for the wedding being in the North was that Edward had just declared peace with Scotland and in the treaty it was agreed that the English kings would give up for all time their claim to a feudal over-lordship of Scotland. The Ragman Rolls were to be returned as well as Scottish heirlooms such as the Royal Regalia, the Stone of Scone and the piece of Christ's cross (the Black Rood).

The Scots agreed to Prince David of Scotland marrying Princess Joan, second daughter of Edward II. King Robert of Scotland would pay England £20,000 in three annual instalments. All the terms were fulfilled, except the return of the Stone of

Scone. When attempts were made to take it from Westminster Abbey, the Londoners rose in rebellion and prevented its removal.

The royal procession moved to Woodstock, one of the King's favourite hunting lodges. It was in these idyllic surroundings that Philippa gave birth to a son, to be named Edward. The year was 1330 and this son would eventually gain great honours for his father, and would be nicknamed 'The Black Prince' from the colour of his armour.

On that day had been born a fair-haired, blue-eyed Prince of Wales of the Plantagenet line. At the Woodstock Palace, a second child was born in 1332, a girl who would be given the name Isabella, after the King's mother. The little princess was to be accorded the privilege of having a cradle for daily use and one for state occasions. Both Prince Edward and Princess Isabella were placed in the care of William St Maur and his wife and they were paid £25 per annum to look after the royal children. Joanna Gaunbar was engaged at a salary of £10 per annum to be rocker of the royal cradles.

A third child was born the following year, a daughter called Joanna. When this child was but two years of age, it was agreed she should marry Frederick, the eldest son of the Duke of Austria and aged five she was taken to the Austrian court to be raised.

However, things did not work out and she was returned to England when she was thirteen and it was agreed she should marry Pedro, the heir to the throne of Castile. In 1348, she arrived in Gascony, only to find the Black Plague was there and she moved to a small village called Loremo, where she unfortunately contracted the plague and died.

Children seemed to be arriving continuously to Edward and Philippa. Edward (the Black Prince) who married Joan of Kent; Isabella, who married the Lord of Coney; Joan, who died of the plague; William who died in infancy; Lionel, who married first Elizabeth de Burgh and then Violanti Visconti; John of Gaunt, who married three times, first to Blanche of Lancaster, then Constanza of Castile and then Joan Holland. Then there was Blanche, who died in infancy; Mary, who married John de Montfort; and Margaret, who married John Hastings, Earl of Pembroke. Another son was born, whom they again named

William, but he too died young. Finally, there was one further son, Thomas, who married Eleanor de Bohun.

It was Edward III who introduced the Order of the Garter as an order of chivalry and he spent lavishly on setting up the order. There seem to be various stories about how the order began, but the sixteenth-century historian Polydor Vergil tells the story that Calais had just fallen into English hands and to celebrate this victory, the King gave a ball at which he expected all the new ladies at the court should dance with the King. Joan, Countess of Salisbury, it is said, dropped her blue garter on the floor and the King, seeing her predicament, came to her assistance and picked up the garter, saying the immortal words, '*Honi soit qui mal y pense*' (Evil be to him who evil thinks). That was the year 1347. The following year, the order was instigated and the first garter ceremony was probably held on 24 June 1348 at Windsor Castle. The order of chivalry still exists with a total of twenty-six knights, including the monarch.

In 1376, tragedy struck the family when Edward, Prince of Wales, was taken ill during battle campaigning in France. The nature of the illness is not certain. It may have been dropsy, dysentery, fever or even cancer, about which the doctors knew nothing then. The prince returned to England, being relieved of his command and being replaced by John of Gaunt. The prince returned to the Manor of Kennington to await his end.

It was on 8 June 1376 (Trinity Sunday) that the Black Prince passed away. He was buried with great pomp at Canterbury Cathedral, a church for which he had a special affection.

King Edward III had indulged in love affairs, but most were short-lived. Alice Perrers was different. She was a strong character and in 1364 she was installed as a Maid of the Queen's Bedchamber. She was awarded the manor of Wendover by the King, plus jewels and two tuns of wine. It seems she was not particularly beautiful, but she had a persuasive tongue. Whether there was anything Queen Philippa could or wanted to do to stop the affair mattered little to the king.

Approximately three years after the affair began, the Queen died of dropsy in 1369 at Windsor. She is buried in Westminster Abbey. She left pensions and gifts to all the women of the bedchamber by name – except Alice Perrers. The King wanted to compensate Alice for her omission from the Queen's will, so he gave her the Queen's jewels. He also had her constantly with him and Parliament voted that she should be banished. Although she did disappear for a time, she came back and was constantly in the King's presence. She was also present when the King was taken ill and she remained until he died in 1377. It is said she removed the rings from his fingers and the medallion around his neck.

King Edward III, who died on 21 June 1377, had reached the age of sixty-five years and had been King for fifty years. He was laid to rest in Westminster Abbey.

Children	Born	Died
Edward	1330	1376 (The Black Prince)
Isabella	1332	1352
Joan	1335	1348
William	1336	1337
Lionel	1338	1368
John	1340	1399
Edmund	1341	1402
Blanche	1342	1342
Mary	1344	1361
Margaret	1346	1361
Thomas	1347	1348
William	1348	1348
Thomas	1355	1397

Anne of Bohemia

1st wife of Richard II
Born 1366
Died 1394
Buried Westminster Abbey

Good Queen Anne

With both his father, the Black Prince, and his grandfather, King
Edward III, dead, Richard became King Richard II in 1377. It was
agreed that the Princess Anne, the daughter of Charles the Holy
Roman Emperor and his wife Elizabeth, should marry Richard.
She was full of charm and grace, but perhaps not to be thought of
as beautiful. Richard loved her from the start and it became an
infatuation.

They were wed at St Stephen's Chapel, Westminster and she
was crowned queen just eight days later and made a member of
the Order of the Garter. She was a perfect wife and only wanted
Richard to be happy. In 1381, during the Peasant's Revolt, Anne
had interceded on behalf of the prisoners and they were released.
She became known as 'Good Queen Anne'.

Richard depended on her and she was an influence for peace
and order. It was because of her intervention that the quarrel
between Richard and the City of London had been patched up. It
seems Richard asked the City for £1,000 but they refused and the
City seemed to resent it when the King arranged to borrow the
money from a Lombardian banker. He was dragged from his
counting house and killed in the street. Richard was furious and
declared that he was going to remove the law courts from London
to York and said he would make York the seat of Parliament.
London could see what these losses would mean, so they pleaded

with the Queen to speak to the King on their behalf; finally he granted the City a pardon.

Suddenly, the queen was taken ill. Although the plague did not seem to be sweeping the country, there were isolated outbreaks from time to time. It was the plague which took her life. She died at Sheen Palace on 7 June 1394. So struck with grief was Richard that he ordered Sheen Palace to be burned to the ground. This was not carried out, but the state apartments were taken down. The King never set foot in that palace again.

Richard was broken hearted, especially at the suddenness of Anne's death. The King made elaborate arrangements for the funeral, importing wax from Flanders to supplement what was already available in this country, to make torches, candles and flambeaux by the thousands. All peers and their wives were commanded to accompany the corpse to the abbey from Sheen Palace.

Two years of sadness passed before Richard reached a decision to marry again. An agreement was signed on 9 March 1396 for him to marry the seven-year-old Isabella, 'The Little Queen'. Her dowry would be a substantial 800,000 francs, to be paid in instalments. The wedding cost £200,000, of which over £7,000 was spent on presents for the French nobility. On 4 November of that year, the marriage took place at Calais. Following the wedding, the Little Queen went to live at Windsor and here she would grow up to be a mature English queen.

Richard was in conflict with Parliament over various issues, including the Peasant Revolt, and the attack on the Earl of Arundel, who arrived late for Queen Anne's funeral. A commission was appointed in 1386 to control the government and so minimise Richard's power. Richard could not accept this and got together a small army, but it was defeated in 1387. Several of Richard's followers were accused of treason and executed, but the King promised to comply with Parliament's wishes and so saved his neck.

He never forgot this episode and, years later, began to take revenge. He executed or exiled his enemies and confiscated their estates. When John of Gaunt died, he seized his lands also. Henry Bolingbroke, John of Gaunt's son, took action with the mighty families of Westmoreland and the Nevilles and the Earl of Northumberland.

Richard was forced into abdication. He was confined to the dungeon of Pontefract Castle where, in 1400, he starved to death or was smothered by his jailer or possibly poisoned.

Richard II, the king who lost his shoe at his coronation, lost his beloved wife so young, lost his friends, lost the trust of the people, lost his throne by abdication and finally his life in a castle dungeon. He was first buried at King's Langley, then moved to Westminster to lie with his first wife, Anne of Bohemia.

Isabella of France

2nd wife of Richard II

Born 1389

Died 1410

Buried Blois St Laumin Abbey
        (Later the remains were moved to
        Church of Celestines, Paris)

The Little Queen

Isabella was the second daughter of Charles VI of France and she was born in Paris. Her mother was Isabella, daughter of Stephen II, Duke of Bavaria-Landshut.

Isabella was only six years of age when Richard proposed. The ambassadors conducting the marriage agreement brought back glowing reports not only of her beauty, but also of her intelligence. At the same time as the marriage agreement was signed, so too was a separate agreement for twenty-eight years of peace.

Richard and Isabella were married at St Nicholas Church, Calais in 1396. 'The Little Queen', aged eight, married Richard to prevent his making a match with a Spanish princess. She loved and adored Richard and after he died in 1400 she refused to consider a marriage to the future Henry V, son of her husband's usurper. She returned to France and in 1406 married her cousin, Charles Duke of Orleans. She died in childbirth in 1410, aged twenty-one.

Historical Background: The House of Lancaster

Henry Bolingbroke assumed the throne as Henry IV on the seizure from his cousin Richard II. There were three major rebellions in Henry's reign. There was also trouble in Wales from Owen Glendower, and the Percys of Northumberland kept him troubled about his northern kingdom. Constant illness plagued Henry and he died in the Jerusalem Chamber of Westminster Abbey in March 1413. Some say he was praying before his departure on a Crusade to Jerusalem.

Henry had patronised Geoffrey Chaucer and John Gower.

The Prince of Wales became Henry V. In 1415, Henry fought the French at Agincourt. It was due to the expertise of the English bowmen that he won the glorious battle on 25 October 1415. Henry V was to be struck down by dysentery and on 31 August 1422 he died. Had he lived just a few short weeks more, he would have been King of France.

Henry VI succeeded his father. He was a religious king, but he was a feeble ruler and watched his country slide into civil war. He was eventually captured at the second Battle of St Albans and finally murdered in the Tower of London three weeks later.

Mary Bohun

1st wife of Henry IV

Born 1369

Died 1394

Buried Leicester
> *(died Peterborough Castle, remains buried Trinity Hospital, Leicester)*

There seemed to be no shortage of heiresses looking for husbands, mainly because many young men were killed in continuous wars. In the latter part of the fourteenth century, there was probably none richer in England than the de Bohun sisters and naturally they would be prime catches.

Humphrey, the tenth Earl of Hereford, who was also Earl of Essex and Northampton, was owner of the Castle of Pleshey in Essex and the castles of Monmouth and Leicester and a house called Cole Harbour in the City of London. On his death, his daughter Eleanor inherited the Essex properties, while Mary, the younger daughter, got the earldoms of Hereford and Leicester, the castle at Monmouth and Cole Harbour.

Eleanor was to marry Thomas of Woodstock. They soon decided that if Mary could eventually be persuaded to take the vow and devote her life to the church, then the property bequeathed to Mary would come to them.

Mary had been placed under the guardianship of John of Gaunt and he said he did not approve of the plan unless Mary fully agreed. Mary did not approve and then fate took a hand in the matter. When she met John of Gaunt's son, Henry, they fell quickly and deeply in love. A marriage was agreed and it proved a very happy one. Mary presented Henry with seven children – four sons and three daughters. It was during the last pregnancy that Mary and the child, a girl, died. Mary had not lived long enough to see her husband become king, but her son Henry, Prince Hal, would eventually become King Henry V.

Due to the deposition of Richard II in Westminster Hall, Richard removed his crown and passed it, along with the sceptre, to Henry. Henry then said, 'I, Henry of Lancaster, challenge the realm of England and the Crown with all the members and appartences, as I am descended by the right line of blood coming from the good lord, Henry II and through that right that God of His Grace hath sent me with the help of my King and of my friends to recover it, the which realm was in point to be undone for default of governance and undoing of good laws.'

It seems he was acclaimed by the Lords and Commons present and so became Henry IV. Henry decided to marry for a second time and his new wife was Joanna of Navarre. Joanna was to start her married life with Henry, but she was not popular with the people. The main reason for this unpopularity was her supposed greed. When she arrived in the country, she brought with her a large retinue of followers, all of whom had to be housed, fed and clothed out of public funds. Her greed also led to her requiring large estates and houses, all of which were grabbed by her, in which the King could see no wrong.

Children	Born	Died
Edward	1382	died aged four days
Henry (V)	1387	1422
Thomas	1388	1413 (killed in battle in France)
John	1389	1435
Humphrey	1390	1447
Blanche	1392	1409
Philippa	1394	1430

Joanna of Navarre

2nd wife of Henry IV
Born 1370
Died 1437
Buried Canterbury Cathedral

Joanna was espoused to John the Valiant, Duke of Brittany. Henry had been invited to the Duke's court while he was in exile. He met and was immediately attracted to Joanna. In 1398, the Duke died and Joanna, in the hope of becoming Henry's second wife, wrote to the Pope. The purpose of the letter was to ask for dispensation to marry again, provided that her new husband was not closer to her in blood than the fourth degree of sanguinity. The Pope gave his dispensation on 20 March 1402. Henry proceeded with the marriage by proxy in 1403. A happy marriage seemed to be certain and she was a devoted wife to Henry.

A committee of the Lords came to a decision that Joanna should reduce her staff considerably and she eventually agreed to keeping only basic staff for herself and her two daughters. This was to consist of two knights, a chambermaid, cook, two chambermaids for her daughters, one mistress, two squires, one messenger and eleven laundresses.

During the King's illness, Joanna cared for her husband like a dutiful wife. He was suffering from leprosy. Henry, in a sudden action while campaigning in the north, allowed the execution of Archbishop Scrope to take place. The archbishop had been accused of leading a rebel force against the king. The reason this shocked the whole country was that it was done quickly and without a formal trial. The day that Archbishop Scrope was executed is the day the King is said to have been stricken with leprosy.

The King said he wanted to die in Jerusalem and preparations were made for the long journey. Before his departure, he went to Westminster Abbey to pray for a safe journey, but was taken ill during his prayers and carried into a small chamber to recover. He never did rally and died on 20 March 1413 in the small room known to this day as the 'Jerusalem Chamber'.

Henry and Joanna of Navarre rest together at Canterbury Cathedral not far from Henry's uncle, the Black Prince. Joanna died in 1437 at Havering-atte-Bower, Essex.

Children: None[1].

---

[1] Joanna had nine children with her first husband, John, Duke of Brittany.

Catherine de Valois

Wife of Henry V
Born 1401
Died 1437
Buried Westminster Abbey

Fair Kate

Catherine de Valois was attractive; thin, with large, brilliant eyes, beautiful hair, but with one Valois feature – the nose. Although it lacked the usual hump – a family trait – it was unmissable. As she stood by Henry in her gown of rich blue velvet, trimmed in ermine and bedecked with jewels, she looked so radiant. She saw Henry for only a short period at the first meeting, but they both fell in love with each other. Shortly after the first meeting, a marriage agreement was drawn up. The couple were married on 2 June 1420 (Trinity Sunday) at the church of St Joan. On their wedding night, Henry was introduced to a French custom. In the middle of the night and without even a knock at the door, the doors of the bridal chamber were thrown open and a parade of court officials carrying candles, followed by royal servants carrying bowls of soup, passed through the room.

The coronation of the Queen took place on 24 February and the succeeding banquet was unusual for one thing – it was Lent and only fish could be served, and it was, in twenty-two different ways.

Catherine went to Windsor. The ladies of the household who would look after the Queen had the names Joanna Belknap, Joanna Troutham and Joanna Coney; they were all named after Henry IV's second wife.

At Windsor, the Queen gave birth to a son, Henry, later Henry

VI. Leaving the newborn child, Katherine journeyed to Harfleur and she met up with an army of 20,000 men under the Duke of Bedford. The Queen was quite shocked to see her husband. He was weak, was of grey complexion, stumbled in his armour and was probably suffering from dysentery. He was sure his strong constitution would be enough to get him over the disease.

Henry died on 31 August 1422. Queen Catherine brought his body back to London. Bishops and abbots followed the coffin through the City. His final resting place would be Westminster Abbey.

The Queen took herself off to one of the dower houses in Baynard's Castle. She was unhappy as a widow and after a suitable period of court mourning, began looking for another husband.

As far as she was concerned, there were three possibilities. John of Bedford, Henry's brother, was handsome enough and she would probably have accepted if he had offered, but John decided the Pope would not agree to him marrying his sister-in-law. Humphrey was another of Henry's brothers, but he was selfish and she had no respect for him. The third choice was Edmund Beaufort, a grandson of John of Gaunt by his third wife.

Catherine may well have preferred the young, sophisticated and handsome knight, but she decided the Pope would not sanction the marriage. Humphrey protested, knowing that if Catherine and Edmund were married, they would be in line for the French regency.

There was another man who came on the scene, one Owen Tudor. He was master of the wardrobe and had occasion to see Katherine about her clothes. It was becoming noticeable he was seeing more of her than his duty demanded.

Over the next ten years of associations, three sons and two daughters were born. By 1428, when the scandal had got out of hand, King Henry VI and Parliament agreed that the Dowager Queen Catherine could not marry anyone without the approval of the King. Eventually, the King decided to bring the matter to a close and he had Owen Tudor arrested and placed in Newgate Prison. Catherine was sent to Bermondsey Abbey.

After two escapes from Newgate, Owen Tudor was finally pardoned and given an annuity. He repaid the King by fighting on the Lancastrian side in the War of the Roses. He was captured at the Battle of Mortimer Cross and beheaded in the market place in Hereford.

Dowager Queen Catherine died at Bermondsey in 1437. Some say she died of an illness; others say it was of a broken heart at having lost Owen Tudor. She was only thirty-six years of age. From this long association with Owen Tudor, of which there seems to have been no formal marriage, came the great house of the Tudors.

Queen Catherine's body was exhumed before the demolition of the old Lady Chapel in Westminster Abbey. Her wooden coffin, wrapped in lead, was placed on the floor of Henry V's Chantry Chapel, where it remained for the next 274 years.

Children	Born	Died
Henry (VI)	1421	1471

Margaret of Anjou

Wife of Henry VI

Born 1430

Died 1482

Buried St Maurice's Cathedral, Angers

Queen of Sorrows

King Henry VI was now twenty-six years of age and as yet unmarried. Not one of the ladies at court had caught his eye. He set his sights, as many had done before him, on the courts of Europe.

He was brought a portrait of a young girl with golden hair and blue eyes and the king decided she was vivacious enough for him and decided to ask for her hand in marriage. She had been born on 23 March 1430, probably at Nancy or Pont-à-Mousson. The portrait was of the French princess, Margaret of Anjou, who came from one of the poorest aristocratic families, because her father was paying off a ransom debt.

Although the princess would have no dowry, the match was arranged when she was just fifteen years of age. She sailed from Harfleur to Portsmouth. When she arrived in England, it was realised that Margaret had very little in the form of a wardrobe. The royal party delayed at Southampton long enough for a suitable wardrobe to be prepared. She then left for London where she was received with great rejoicing and her emblem, the daisy, was worn in the caps of all the citizens. The King was so in love with his new queen he would do anything for her and immediately started a major redecorating of the royal palaces.

They were married in Westminster Abbey and this was followed by two days of tournaments and feasting. A child was born on 13 October 1453, a son to be named Edward. The country should now be rejoicing, but people had become suspicious of the Queen after the mysterious death of Duke Humphrey. Rumours were spreading that the newborn child was not the King's but that of Edmund Beaufort, Duke of Somerset. Others were saying the Queen's child had died and a child of a lowly family had been placed in the royal cradle.

The King was not able to proclaim the son as his legitimate heir as he was suffering a mental illness and was in a coma. Rumours were also spreading that the King was dying. Parliament now had the dilemma of a king who could not rule and an heir too young to rule. A regent would have to be appointed, and Richard of York was elected.

By Christmas, the King showed signs of recovery. Queen Margaret took their son to him and he was pleased to recognise the boy and approve of his name.

The country was now in the midst of civil war with the red rose of Lancaster fighting the white rose of York. During one of the battles, the King was taken prisoner and confined in the Tower. The Queen had fled to France, fleeing from the Yorkist army. At the Battle of Tewkesbury, young Prince Edward was killed and the Queen, who returned to England to fight her husband's cause, was captured at the same battle. She too was taken to the Tower and the day she arrived her husband, Henry VI, died in the Wakefield Tower – some say from grief and illness, others say he was murdered. The year was 1461. The King was dead, the Queen was in prison and the heir to the throne had been slaughtered in battle.

The King's body was put on display at Blackfriars before being taken to Chertsey for burial. When the Queen was released from prison, the years of imprisonment had taken their toll. She was now middle-aged, her hair streaked with grey and her face well lined.

She was asked to sign the following formal declaration:

I, Margaret, formerly in England married, renounce all that I could pretend to in England by the condition of my marriage with all other things these to Edward now King of England.

The Queen proceeded into exile to Reculée near Angers. Several years she stayed there. She was now almost a recluse, walking in the gardens of the Castle of Dampierre, to which she had moved with her staff.

On 2 August 1482, Margaret of Anjou made her will, leaving her few possessions to her staff and few friends.

This once-beautiful princess from humble beginnings, who became Queen of England, produced an heir, yet was to lose all and finish in solitude. She finally died on 25 August 1482 and was buried in Angers Cathedral, but her tomb was destroyed during the French Revolution.

She was responsible for founding Queen's College, Cambridge.

The King married Margaret at St Martin, Tours in 1444 by proxy and then in person in 1443 at Titchfield Abbey, Hants.

Children	Born	Died
Edward	1463	1471 (killed in battle at Tewkesbury)

Historical Background: The House of York

Edward IV was descended from Lionel, second son of Edward III. The War of the Roses, which had begun in 1455 and was to continue for thirty years, with only twelve weeks of actual fighting, was over the right of the throne – whether it should be a Lancastrian or a Yorkist king. Edward's was to be a troubled reign with supporters of Henry VI, including his wife Queen Margaret, trying to win back the throne.

In 1476, printing from moveable type came to England, brought by William Caxton, and remained at Westminster until 1491, when Caxton died and the presses were moved by Wynkyn de Worde, who moved them to Fleet Street.

Edward IV died of a fever in 1483 and his great misfortune was that he died having two young sons, too young to rule in his place.

Edward V, although named as his father's successor, lived only two months and was never crowned. He was murdered with his brother Richard, Duke of York, in the Bloody Tower of the Tower of London in 1483.

The person to succeed young Edward was Richard III, brother of the late Edward IV. His would also be a short reign of two and a half years, before he lost his life at the Battle of Bosworth Field in 1485. So this brought to an end the War of the Roses. The crown, which had been thrown by Richard into a thorn bush, was recovered and Henry of Lancaster was proclaimed king by virtue of his victory on the battlefield and by agreement with Parliament. So, in the year of 1485, began the great age of the Tudors.

Elizabeth Woodville

Wife of Edward IV
Born 1437
Died 1492
Buried St George's Chapel, Windsor

The Grey Mare

Elizabeth, daughter of Sir Richard Woodville, had been married to John Grey, son of Earl Ferrers. He fought on the side of the Lancastrians, but died of wounds at the Battle of St Albans in 1455 and she was left with two sons, Richard and Thomas. When Edward IV became king, he confiscated the Ferrers estates, leaving Elizabeth without support. She became one of the ladies of the bedchamber to Margaret of Anjou. Edward, out hunting one day, first set eyes on Elizabeth and fell in love. He tried to convince Elizabeth he was serious, but she said, 'Full well enough I know I am not good enough to be your queen, but dear liege Lord I am far too good to be a mistress.'

On 1 May 1464 they were married at Grafton Regis, Northants. Edward then announced to the court he was married and Elizabeth Woodville was declared Queen. She was crowned Queen in Westminster Abbey on 26 May 1465. There were those at court who were not happy about the situation. Elizabeth's brothers and sisters accompanied her to court. They were all looking for suitable partners in marriage. Her sister Mary married William Herbert, later Earl of Pembroke, and her brother John married the eighty-year-old dowager Duchess of Norfolk.

Elizabeth's father was created an Earl, at that time considered a very high rank, the backbone of the nobility – the higher rank of Duke being reserved for those of royal blood. The peers were now not just unhappy, but their anger had grown to a fever pitch.

The Earl of Warwick, 'The Kingmaker', saw his power in the land decreasing and so began scheming. The King's brother George, Duke of Clarence, named George after the patron saint of England and the first member of the Royal Family to bear that name, could, with planning, be made King, and he would be easily manipulated by Warwick. To gain George's support to his plan, he married George off to his daughter, Isabel.

The Earl of Warwick got support from the King of France, Louis XI, and it was agreed an army would cross to England and take the throne from Edward. Things went drastically wrong for the Kingmaker's army at the Battle of Barnet in 1471. Richard Neville, the Earl of Salisbury as well as Warwick were all cut down and killed.

Elizabeth Woodville now felt the throne to be safely back in the hands of Edward. She bore the King ten children of whom only three emerge as historically important. Although things seemed to be in a state of happy married bliss, the Woodvilles were no better liked.

The King's brother, George, who might have become king if Warwick's plan had succeeded at the Battle of Barnet, was still a threat. So, George, Duke of Clarence, was arrested and confined to the Tower. A long list of charges was read out, including treason, murder of two of his servants and that he spread rumours that King Edward was illegitimate. He was sentenced to death for these charges. The King did not want a public spectacle made of George's death, so he was drowned in a butt of Malmsey wine. A butt held 120 gallons and the wine came from Morea in Greece. It was a strong and sweet variety. Evidence does not prove any other explanation about George's death. It is even said he chose his death himself.

King Edward IV was suffering bad health. He was getting fat and flabby. He had given up going hunting and spent each evening drinking himself into a stupor. He died on 9 April 1483 and was buried at St George's Chapel, Windsor. Edward and Elizabeth's son, Edward, was proclaimed Edward V, but his reign was brief, that of only two months.

The mystery of the death of Edward V and his brother

Richard, Duke of York is still being argued over. The young king was supposedly taken to the Tower for his safety. Richard, his brother, and their mother Elizabeth had sought sanctuary in Westminster Abbey. The queen was persuaded that Richard would be safer in the Tower with his brother. That was the last they were seen alive. Dr Shaw, Richard of Gloucester's chaplain, appeared at St Paul's Cross and attempted to prove that Elizabeth's marriage to Edward IV was not legitimate, as Edward had been betrothed to Lady Eleanor Talbot before he married Elizabeth. This would mean the young princes were illegitimate.

Elizabeth Woodville was sent to the abbey at Bermondsey in 1486 and it was here she died six years later on 10 April 1492.

Edward had, like many Plantagenets before him, been lavish when it came to spending money. He had a very costly stable built and men would pass comments by saying 'the princely stables and the favourite grey mare'. This was a play on the Queen's original marriage to John Grey, Earl Ferrers of Groby.

Elizabeth Woodville died at Bermondsey Abbey in 1492 and was buried beside her husband at Windsor's St George's Chapel.

Children[1]	Born	Died
Elizabeth	1466	1503
Mary	1467	1482
Cecilia	1469	1507
Edward (V)	1470	1483 (murdered in Tower)
Margaret	1472	1472
Richard	1473	1483 (murdered in Tower)
Anne	1475	1511
George	1477	1479
Katherine	1479	1527
Bridget	1480	1517

[1] Edward IV also had at least four illegitimate children.

Anne Neville

Wife of Richard III
Born 1456
Died 1485
Buried Westminster Abbey

Daughter of the Kingmaker

Warwick the Kingmaker, otherwise Richard Neville, Earl of Warwick, was the chief supporter in the bid by Richard, Duke of Gloucester to become King Richard III. Warwick had two most charming and attractive daughters, Isobel and Anne. When Richard first met them, they were only children and certainly there were not thoughts of marriage. The Kingmaker was a clever and ambitious man and he would use his daughters to further these ambitions. Isobel was eventually to marry George, Duke of Clarence, but that marriage was not to last long, for Isobel died quite young, probably of consumption.

Anne, now aged thirteen, was taken to France. Her father would change sides and fight to replace Henry VI on the throne and she would be married to Edward, Prince of Wales. Some say the marriage took place immediately. It is more likely the marriage would have had to wait until the Kingmaker had fulfilled his promise to replace Henry on the throne. This he did, taking Edward IV by surprise; Richard escaped to Holland.

Richard could not have been very happy. He was not in exile and the girl he wanted to marry was going to marry the heir to the Lancastrian throne. However, Edward IV returned to fight and the Kingmaker was killed at the Battle of Barnet in 1471. Young Prince Edward was killed at the Battle of Tewkesbury, also in 1471.

Anne was placed under the care of the Duke of Cambridge. There were all sort of romantic stories going around that Richard searched for her everywhere and finally found her working as a kitchen servant.

How and where Richard found Anne is of no consequence, but when they did meet again, Richard had her moved to the sanctuary of St Martin-le-Grand, and shortly afterwards they were married.

During the rest of Edward IV's reign, Richard and Anne settled in the north of England at Middleham Castle in Wensleydale. Here, in 1474, a son was born and named Edward.

On the death of Edward IV in 1483, yet another Edward succeeded as Edward V. Edward and his brother Richard were murdered in the Tower, which in itself is a long and complicated story and historians will probably argue until the end of time about who was the guilty party. Was it their Uncle Richard? Certainly, by their disappearance and ultimate murder, Richard became King Richard III.

If all Richard had to do was to get rid of the two sons of Edward IV, the whole story might be more feasible – but what about the others in line for the throne? There were Edward's five daughters and the Duke of Clarence's son and daughter. Richard himself had three elder sisters and one of them had a son. That's eleven other contenders to be considered. There were plots and counterplots, murder, charges of conspiracy and treason going from one side to the other, which makes the whole tragedy a deep and mysterious story.

Anne, Richard's wife, was not in good health and perhaps he wanted to be able to place a crown on her head before she died. She would then know her frail son would be heir to the throne. In 1484, Richard was journeying through the northern counties and on arrival in Nottingham he was told his son had died. With great speed, he returned to Middleham Castle with a saddened heart, not only because of his son's death, but also because he died alone with neither parent present. It was a devastating blow to Anne, still not a fit woman. She spent Christmas with Richard at Westminster, but early the following year, on 16 March, she passed away.

Rumours began that Richard had poisoned his wife in order to marry the daughter of Edward IV, the young Princess Elizabeth.

Richard was crowned in 1483, but it was a short reign. At the coronation, Anne's train was carried by the tall, slender figure of Margaret Beaufort, Countess of Richmond and Derby, mother of Henry VII and grandmother of Henry VIII. Had the Tudors already got their foot inside the door?

Richard's son and wife were now dead and it was not long before the Tudors showed their strength at the Battle of Bosworth in 1485 – despite the courage of Richard III, who grabbed a battleaxe and rode straight into a cluster of Henry's army, where he was cut down.

On that day in 1485 ended the War of the Roses. Richard lay dead on the battlefield and the crown that Richard had been wearing was recovered from the thorn bush and placed on Henry's head. So ended the Plantagenet line and so began the line of the illustrious Tudors. Henry was now Henry VII and a king by conquest. Anne died of tuberculosis.

Children[1]	Born	Died
Edward	1473	1484

---

[1] Richard had at least seven illegitimate children.

Historical Background: The Tudors

Henry VII had claimed his crown by conquest, agreement with Parliament and his marriage to Elizabeth of York. Henry was a wise king and on his death left the country stable and financially very secure. During his reign, Columbus discovered the Bahamas in 1492. By 1497, John Cabot had discovered Labrador. In 1499, Vasco da Gama rounded the Cape of Good Hope to discover the sea route to India. In 1499, Amerigo Vespucci explored the coast of South America. It was an age of discovery.

Henry VII was to lose his eldest son Arthur; young Henry became Henry VIII. Henry VIII, apart from his matrimonial problems, which are outlined in the section on queens, was a defender of the Church. In 1521, Pope Leo X conferred on Henry the title Defender of the Faith for his defence of the seven sacraments against Martin Luther, the sermon reformer.

During this period, the suppression of the monasteries began the breakaway from the Church in Rome and the setting up of the Church of England, with Henry making himself supreme head. Henry died in 1547, having been king for thirty-eight years. He was fifty-five years of age and was survived by two of his wives, Anne of Cleves and Catherine Parr.

Edward VI, 'the boy king', assumed the throne aged ten and a half years of age and was a sickly child from birth. The country was virtually ruled by the Duke of Somerset on Edward's death from consumption in 1553, aged sixteen. Mary Tudor (Mary I) was to succeed.

There appeared, however, Lady Jane Grey, who had no wish to become queen, but was being used as a pawn by her husband, Lord Guilford Dudley; her father-in-law, the Duke of Northumberland; and the Duke of Suffolk, her father. All four were to be executed for high treason when Mary Tudor, daughter of Henry VIII and Catherine of Aragon, became queen.

Mary Tudor's reign was to be a rather short one of five years. The Roman Catholic religion was brought back – the act of being a heretic brought the death penalty, usually by burning, and some 283 martyrs died this way at Smithfield alone.

Mary married Philip II of Spain but there were no children. She died in 1553.

Elizabeth, Mary I's half-sister – daughter of Anne Boleyn – became Queen and so began the Elizabethan age, which lasted for forty-five years. The Protestant religion was restored. A year after Elizabeth's accession began, there were attempts to get Mary, Queen of Scots on to the throne. There were many plots, including the Ridolfi, Throckmorton and the Babington plot, but none succeeded.

Eventually, Mary, Queen of Scots, the unfortunate Queen, was executed at Fotheringay Castle on 8 February 1587. A year later, the Spanish Armada attempted to gain the throne for Philip of Spain and avenge the death of Mary, Queen of Scots.

This, too, was the age of Shakespeare.

During the period of Elizabeth's reign, there were attempts at colonisation of Newfoundland, Virginia and Guiana. The East India Company was founded in 1600. The country was at peace and although Elizabeth had many suitors, she remained unmarried.

She died at the age of almost seventy in 1603, leaving the country in the hands of James VI of Scotland, son of Mary, Queen of Scots. And so began the Stuart age!

Elizabeth of York

Wife of Henry VII
Born 1466
Died 1503
Buried Westminster Abbey

The Face of a Queen on a Pack of Cards

Turmoil and intrigue surrounded the death of the young princes in the tower, the boys Edward and Richard, Duke of York, who were the brothers of Elizabeth of York. Elizabeth, the eldest daughter of Edward IV and Elizabeth Woodville, was betrothed to the Dauphin of France in 1475 but his father, Louis XI, broke off the proposed match in 1482. Elizabeth, engaged at nine, was now free again at the age of seventeen. Shortly after Edward IV died she was suggested as a bride for Henry Tudor (Henry VII), but Henry did not marry immediately, largely because he did not want it to appear that he owed his crown to his wife's superior claim.

The couple were finally married on 18 January 1486 at Westminster. Elizabeth was a radiant bride, tall and of considerable beauty, with a fair complexion and long golden tresses. She was to have seven children for Henry, of whom three survived her. Margaret, who would marry the future James IV of Scotland, was born 1489; Henry, later Henry VIII, born 1491; and Mary, born 1495, was married briefly to Louis XII of France and then married Charles Brandon, Duke of Suffolk. There was a boy, Arthur, who was married to Catherine of Aragon, but he died at the age of fifteen.

Elizabeth of York could not have had better connections, for she was daughter of a king (Edward IV), sister of a king (Edward

V), she married a king (Henry VII), gave birth to a king (Henry VIII) and was niece of a king (Richard III). She was also mother-in-law of the kings of Scotland and France and was also the grandmother of Edward VI, Mary I and Elizabeth I.

Henry VII was not a chivalrous or romantic person; his virtues were patience and diplomacy. Henry was the first of a new dynasty and after the civil war was determined to establish the Tudors and achieve a national recovery. His achievements included avoiding bankruptcy and war and raising the revenue from the known estates by forty per cent. He may well have got the name of being a miser but he did buy a leopard for the Tower menagerie and on one day paid John van Delf £38 1s 4d for garnishing a salad.

The death of Henry and Elizabeth's son Arthur was a severe blow, particularly for Elizabeth; she was ill, and a month after Arthur's funeral she was once again pregnant. She chose to give birth to this child in the royal apartments at the Tower of London. It was here in February 1503 she died after giving birth to a baby girl. The baby was christened quickly and given the name of Catherine, but the baby died a few days later.

Elizabeth of York was just thirty-seven years of age. From the Tower her body was conveyed in a great and solemn procession through the city, with her effigy in royal robes with crown and sceptre. There were eight ladies of the court following on white horses and a procession of clergy, the Lord Mayor and Commonalty of the city of London.

Elizabeth had been the last of the House of York to wear the crown of England and she had given birth to two Princes of Wales, one who became Henry VIII. She will be remembered for centuries to come as Elizabeth who first appeared as the Queen on a pack of playing cards in 1492 and she has remained there for over 500 years.

Children Born Died

Arthur	1486	1502 (Married Catherine of Aragon but he died aged 15)

Margaret	1489	1541 (Married King James IV of Scotland)
Henry (VIII)	1491	1547
Elizabeth	1492	1495
Mary	1495	1573 (Married King Louis XII of France but he died three months later. She then married Charles Brandon, Duke of Suffolk)
Edmund	1499	1500
Edward		died young
Catherine	1503	1503 (Queen Elizabeth of York died in childbirth and the child did not survive)

Elizabeth of York – Royal Connections

Father – Edward IV	King 1461–1483 (York)
Brother – Edward V	King 1483 (York)
Uncle – Richard III	King 1483–1485 (York)
Husband – Henry VII	King 1485–1509 (Tudor)
Son Henry – VIII	King 1509–1547 (Tudor)
Grandson – Edward VI	King 1547–1553 (Tudor)
Granddaughter – Mary I	Queen 1553–1588 (Tudor)
Granddaughter – Elizabeth I	Queen 1558–1603 (Tudor)
Granddaughter – Mary	Queen of Scotland
Granddaughter – Margaret	Queen of France

Catherine of Aragon

1st wife of Henry VIII
Born 1485
Died 1536
Buried Peterborough Cathedral

Wife to a Prince of Wales and a King

Henry, second son of Henry VII had not expected to become King of England – he had an older brother, Arthur. Henry VII was looking for a wife for Arthur when Arthur was but two years of age. He was a handsome young lad but he was not particularly strong. When he reached the age of ten he was to be married to Catherine of Aragon at St Paul's Cathedral, but within four months of the marriage Arthur had died.

The little Spanish princess, fourth daughter of King Ferdinand and Queen Isabelle, had come to a strange country to be married at the age of sixteen on 14 November 1501. On arrival in England for the wedding she was escorted by an archbishop and a bishop plus a large troop of duennas – Spanish etiquette was demanded, which meant neither Prince Arthur nor King Henry VII could see the bride before the wedding. The King decided this could not be and he and Arthur rode over to the Spanish camp and demanded to see Catherine. The Spaniards agreed and all sat down to supper together.

Catherine, dark skinned and vivacious, was duly married at St Paul's in November of 1501 and by 2 April 1502 she was a widow when Arthur died of consumption. Only two and a half months later she was betrothed to Henry (25 June) and married him in 1509, seven weeks after Henry became King.

Between 1510 and 1518 she had five children, all of whom

died except a girl, who would grow up and become Queen of England as Mary Tudor ('Bloody Mary').

Henry, now King Henry VIII, was a handsome and accomplished ruler. He could speak French, Latin, English and a little Italian and German. He could play the lute and harpsichord, sing, draw the bow with greater strength than probably any man in the kingdom and he was excellent at the joust.

Henry and Catherine seemed to be an ideal match. She responded to his youthful looks and strong personality; they were certainly in love. Catherine gave birth to a son on New Year's Day 1511 and the King was overjoyed. He organised a great tournament to celebrate the occasion and it rivalled the celebration of the King's coronation. The boy was christened Henry but in less than two months he died. Only ten years later Henry ceased to be a loving husband, but Catherine remained a loyal and devoted wife. As loving as she was, however, she had not been able to produce a son and heir.

Henry did not know why he was denied a son and he did not place the blame solely on Catherine. Perhaps, he thought, he had offended God and he found part of the answer, he believed, in the Bible:

> Thou shalt not uncover the nakedness of thy brother's wife: it is thy brother's nakedness.
>
> Leviticus 17:18

and also:

> If a man shall take his brother's wife, it is an unclean thing: he hath uncovered his brother's nakedness, they shall be childless.
>
> Leviticus 20:21

Although this was directed at those who committed adultery, Henry believed this was reason enough. Henry now wanted a divorce. He was being spurred on by Anne Boleyn. Cardinal Wolsey could not see how he could get a divorce after all these years.

On 1 June 1527 news reached London that Emperor Charles, Catherine of Aragon's nephew, had taken over Rome and made the Pope a virtual prisoner. Cardinal Wolsey realised there was no point in pursuing the matter of a divorce with Catherine's nephew in charge of affairs in the Vatican. It was, however, possible that the imprisoned Pope Clement VII could be persuaded to delegate his power to Cardinal Wolsey and he could then annul Henry's marriage. News got back to Emperor Charles, who naturally gave his support to Queen Catherine.

A protracted hearing took place at Blackfriars with Cardinal Wolsey and Cardinal Campeggio, the papal legate, but nothing was achieved. Henry was getting extremely impatient and it was not long before Wolsey was deposed. The Cardinal had intended to go to York but got only as far as Leicester where he died on 29 November 1530.

Henry was a devout Catholic. He had been honoured by the Pope in 1521, receiving the title 'Defender of the Faith' for his book defending the Catholic faith against the treatment of the sacrament by Martin Luther.

Eventually the break from Rome would have to come to enable Henry to marry a second wife. The Archbishop of Canterbury, Thomas Cranmer, declared that Henry and Catherine had not been husband and wife. Catherine now accepted defeat and retired first to Amphill, Bedfordshire and then to Kimbolton Castle, Huntingdonshire, where she lived until her death from cancer in 1536 aged fifty-one years. She was laid to rest in Peterborough Cathedral.

Children	*Born*	*Died*
Unnamed child	1510	stillborn
Henry	1511	died fifty-two days later
Miscarriage	1511	
Unnamed son	1513	lived only a few hours
Henry	1514	lived only a few hours
Mary Tudor	1516	1558
Miscarriage	1517	
Unnamed daughter	1518	stillborn

Anne Boleyn

2nd wife of Henry VIII
Born 1507
Died 1536
Buried St Peter ad Vincula, Tower of London

Anne of a Thousand Days

Anne Boleyn, Henry VIII's second wife, had been a lady-in-waiting at the royal court for several years and Henry was infatuated by her. She was considered to be extremely handsome rather than beautiful. She had a swarthy complexion, long neck, wide mouth and it seemed an almost perfect body. Anne was the daughter of Thomas Boleyn and his wife, Elizabeth, daughter of the 2nd Duke of Norfolk.

Anne owed her presence at court to her sister, Mary. When Anne returned from a period in France as a lady-in-waiting to the Queen of France she found her sister enjoying all the royal favours.

When Henry first made advances towards Anne he was most surprised to find that she would not follow the way of her sister or the King's former mistress Beatrice Blount. If Henry wanted her that badly he would get her only by making her an honest woman. Anne then decided to leave court and return to Hever Castle, the family home in Kent. Letters soon began to arrive at the castle for Anne and Henry was pouring out his love and affection. Henry's history may have taken a completely different course if he had not met Anne; Bessie Blount, Henry's previous mistress had produced a son, Henry Fitzroy, now six years of age and created the Duke of Richmond and Somerset. Henry was now considering that if he could not be succeeded by a legitimate male heir, then the throne could perhaps go to his illegitimate son.

Meeting Anne was a turning point; he now wanted a divorce. A divorce would not be obtained easily but Anne was prepared to wait and she did for six years. In 1532 Henry created her the Marquess of Pembroke (not the Marchioness) and this was the first title to be created for a woman to hold in her own right.

Anne became pregnant and on 25 January 1533 she and Henry were married at York Place, Whitehall. On 31 May 1533 Anne was crowned Queen in a great ceremony in Westminster Abbey. Henry had spent lavishly on the ceremony and Anne had achieved her ambition. As the coronation procession passed through the streets Anne noticed that few doffed their hats in respect and the whole day seemed to be much more solemn than previous coronations.

Shortly before four o'clock on Sunday, 7 September 1533 a girl was born to Anne and named Elizabeth (the future Elizabeth I). She was born at Greenwich and was a healthy child. The christening took place at the church of the Franciscan at Greenwich and although the Lord Mayor and Aldermen of the city attended in full regalia Henry VIII did not attend. He was perhaps showing his disappointment that the child was not a boy!

Elizabeth Barton, 'The Holy Maid of Kent', was making pronouncements in public that if Henry married Anne Boleyn he would die within nine months. Other opponents of the divorce from Catherine of Aragon and the marriage to Anne Boleyn were also making open statements. Bishop John Fisher and Dr Edward Bocking were but two of these. Elizabeth Barton was being encouraged by the people and she was becoming something of a local Joan of Arc. As one would expect she was arrested and paraded around the streets and out on display at St Paul's Cathedral as a form of ridicule. She was then sent to prison from where, in April of 1534, she was, along with Dr Edward Bocking, taken to Tyburn and hanged. Bishop John Fisher had only just escaped through lack of evidence.

The bishop was treading a dangerous path and was seeking from Emperor Charles material support in the form of an army to depose Henry. He had spoken openly in defence of Queen

Catherine of Aragon and was finally arrested and taken to the Tower where his friend Sir Thomas More followed him two days later. They had fought a lonely campaign and had refused to submit to Henry's command to sign the Act of Succession, thus declaring Mary Tudor illegitimate and the children of Henry and Anne the heirs to the throne.

Help from Rome did not seem to be forthcoming, but there was a turn of events when a new Pope was elected. He was Pope Paul III and he announced his intention of creating Bishop John Fisher a Prince of the Roman Catholic Church – a Cardinal.

Henry was furious and said he would help the Pope bestow the honour personally by sending him Fisher's head – then he could place the Cardinals' hat on it himself.

On 22 June 1535 Bishop John Fisher was executed followed by Sir Thomas More on 6 July 1535. Early the following year Catherine of Aragon died in January 1536. When Henry heard of her death he and Anne Boleyn dressed themselves completely in bright yellow and attended a Mass followed by a banquet and jousting tournament. On the day that Catherine of Aragon was buried at Peterborough Cathedral, 27 January, Anne Boleyn had a miscarriage. Some thought this to be divine judgement. Anne, however, declared that the miscarriage was due to the shock she received from hearing that Henry had had a bad fall from his horse during the joust.

The love Henry originally had for Anne had been cooling since the birth of Elizabeth. Sir Thomas More once said during his captivity in the Tower, 'Anne might scorn our heads off like footballs, but it will not be long before her head will dance the little dance.'

It was being left to Archbishop Cranmer and the Duke of Norfolk to make investigations into rumours about Anne's conduct with various men. A list was drawn up of those who had committed adultery with the Queen; this included her own brother, Lord Rochford. She was duly arrested and tried before twenty-six people of the realm, the trial presided over by the Duke of Norfolk, her uncle. Four of those named on the list, Norris, Weston, Breeton and Smeaton, were also tried. Only Mark Smeaton had confessed, under torture. They were all executed on 17 March 1536. Anne was also found guilty. She was executed inside the precincts of the Tower on 19 May 1536, being beheaded by a sword and not an axe. The sword and swordsman were brought over especially from St Omer in France. This was the only time this type of execution had been carried out in this country.

The moment Henry found out Anne was dead he boarded his barge and went to call on Jane Seymour.

Anne, who had not wanted to become a king's mistress like her sister Mary, had waited six years for the divorce from Catherine of Aragon to have only three short years as Queen. She was now dead and forgotten. Her daughter, Elizabeth, would one day become a great Tudor queen despite Henry's insistence that a woman would not be strong enough to rule. Anne Boleyn's daughter would be queen for almost forty-five years and bring the Tudor dynasty to a close.

Children	*Born*	*Died*
Elizabeth	1533	1603
Stillborn child	1534	
Miscarriage	1535	
Stillborn child	1536	

Jane Seymour

3rd wife of Henry VIII
Born 1509
Died 1537
Buried St George's Chapel, Windsor

Plain Jane

Almost immediately after Anne Boleyn gave birth to Elizabeth, Henry was falling out of love with her. His affections were turning to one of Anne's ladies-in-waiting, Jane Seymour.

A modest and somewhat shy girl, daughter of Sir John Seymour and Margaret (daughter of Sir Henry Wentworth of Wolf Hall in Wiltshire), Jane was not particularly interested in Henry's attention to her. She returned his letters unopened; she spurned a purse of gold, and made him promise to speak to her only in the presence of others. Sir Edward Seymour, her brother, was, however, much more ambitious. Thomas Cromwell was ejected from his quarters so that Jane's brother could occupy them.

Although Jane was shy and acted the part, this just made Henry all the more eager to get her. Jane's character was one of an honest and straightforward girl, who was pretty but not one might call a dazzling beauty, Time would show that Henry was sincere in his approaches to Jane. In 1536 Anne Boleyn was executed and as soon as Henry heard she was dead he set out to visit Jane. By the end of the month of May 1536 he was married to her.

The production of a male heir was still Henry's main thought and he wasted no time with Jane to try again. Henry was now forty-five, so time was not on his side. He therefore decided to confer the succession on any children of Jane's.

Jane was also planning a reconciliation between Henry and his daughter Mary – she was accepted back to court. Elizabeth was already there. She was just three years old and Mary was twenty, so here was a united Royal Family once again.

On 12 October 1537 it was announced that Queen Jane at the Palace of Hampton had given birth to a son. Henry was now overjoyed; his ten-year battle with the Papacy was finally blessed as Henry had wanted. Henry returned immediately from Esher and decided his son should be called Edward, for that was his great-grandfather's name, and it was St Edward's Day when the news reached Henry.

Three wives, a breakaway from the Church in Rome, a wife divorced and a wife executed – and now his dream of a son and heir to succeed him and continue the Tudor line had come true. But at what price! And now at Hampton Court his dear, sweet Jane, who had realised his dearest ambition, was dying. Jane had undergone surgery to release the child and this caused her to have puerperal fever. She lingered for twelve days and then died.

Henry, who had been in a state of joyous trance, was now devastated by Jane's death. He loved her, for she had given him his son.

Jane's body lay in state for three weeks and she was conveyed a magnificent funeral with all the pomp of such a solemn occasion. The body was conveyed to St George's Chapel, Windsor. Jane was possibly the only one of his wives he really loved and it was by her side he would be buried when he died. There were still three more wives to come but none would take the place of dear Jane.

Children	Born	Died
Edward (VI)	1537	1553

Anne of Cleves

4th wife of Henry VIII
Born 1515
Died 1557
Buried Westminster Abbey

The Flanders Mare

The death in 1537 of Jane Seymour was a bitter blow to Henry. By 1539 it was suggested he should marry again. Young Prince Edward was not a very healthy child. Another marriage might produce another male heir as a safeguard for the realm. It was considered that Henry might look to the house of Cleves.

By March 1539 Thomas Cromwell was advising the king that Princess Anne of Cleves was of incomparable beauty; and certainly she was more beautiful than Christine, the Duchess of Milan, who had been considered as possible wife. Hans Holbein had gone to Brussels in 1538 to paint Anne's portrait. Henry might well have married her, for she was beautiful according to the portrait, but she was a widow and Henry would require Papal dispensation.

Anne of Cleves was daughter of John III, Duke of Cleves and Mary, daughter of William III, Duke of Jülich-Cleves-Berg. Anne had a sister, Amelia, who was also being considered by Henry. It was Anne whom Henry decided upon, but he was not pleased with the actual product. He went to Rochester to meet her as he wanted a secret glimpse. Henry told Cromwell that she was nothing so well as she was spoken of.

The marriage was postponed for two days. This gave Henry time to think of how he could get rid of his bride-to-be, his 'Flanders Mare'.

Anne was daughter of the Duke of Cleves, who was part of the Schmalkaldic League – a league of princes of Germany who would assist each other against the Emperor Charles of France. It was important to Henry to have allies against the French. Henry realised he could not afford to upset his German allies. So for these reasons the marriage took place and he also went to bed with Anne. The following day the King said he had left her as good a maid as he had found her.

After a short period of six months divorce proceedings were started. Anne seemed to be quietly and meekly agreeing to the divorce. It was agreed the marriage had not been consummated. It was a very orderly end to a brief and loveless marriage. Anne stated it was her wish to stay in England and had several country properties given to her.

Anne had not suffered unduly from the quick divorce; Thomas Cromwell on the other hand was arrested on 10 June 1540. Cromwell was blamed for producing the flattering portrait of Anne which had placed Henry in a compromising position.

It was not just the portrait Henry complained about but the accompanying notes put forward by Thomas Cromwell. They had been edited in such a way as to give Henry a glowing report about Anne of Cleves that Cromwell knew to be untrue.

Thomas Cromwell, Lord Chancellor of England and Vicar Seminal, would pay the price by being executed at Tower Hill.

Anne of Cleves lived until 1557 some ten years after Henry's death in 1547. She was buried in Westminster Abbey.

Children: None.

Catherine Howard

5th wife of Henry VIII

Born 1521

Died 1542

Buried St Peter ad Vincula, Tower of London

The Queen and the Love Affair

The Norfolk family, who had helped strip Cromwell of his power, now played another game. With Anne of Cleves divorced from Henry VIII the Duke of Norfolk's niece was being pushed forward as a possible fifth wife. She too was in the royal household as a maid of honour. Catherine Howard was the daughter of Lord Edmund Howard and Joyce, daughter of Sir Richard Culpepper.

It was a busy summer in 1540: Anne of Cleves and Henry were divorced, Cromwell was executed and Katherine and Henry were married. It had been thought for a period in 1538 that Henry was near the end of his life because of a wound that had been drained and caused a blood clot in his lungs. For a whole week Henry was unable to speak and black in the face.

Now it was 1540, and with Catherine by his side he seemed in much better health and very happy.

He showered his teenage queen with gifts including the estate of Jane Seymour and house of Thomas Cromwell, and he also gave her gifts of diamonds, rubies, emeralds and pearls. She befriended Anne of Cleves, who was now being regarded as the King's sister. Catherine had risen to a majestic position so quickly and almost as quickly would she fall. As Catherine's mother had died when she was just ten years of age she was placed in the care of the Dowager Duchess of Norfolk and more or less left unchaperoned. She was soon getting involved in secret love affairs.

During one of Henry's royal progresses in 1541 she was secretly meeting Thomas Culpeper, aided and abetted by Jane, Viscountess Rochford, her lady-in-waiting. They were playing a dangerous game. Finally, one John Lascelles, who had information from his sister about the Queen's secret meetings, told the King. He refused to believe the rumours.

The Archbishop of Canterbury, Thomas Cranmer, told the King the details. As he could not bring himself to do it face to face he wrote instead a long letter.

Manox, Catherine's music teacher, confessed; so did Francis Dereham, her cousin, to association with the Queen before her marriage to the King. It was Lady Rochford who said that Culpeper and the queen had known each other carnally, considering what she had heard and seen. She had not only condemned Culpeper but also herself, for conspiracy.

By the end of that year in 1541 both Dereham and Culpepper were executed. Queen Catherine and Lady Rochford were to be put to death the following year in 1542, despite the Queen's pleas that she was innocent. On the scaffold when she made her final speech, she said, 'Today I die the Queen of England, but rather I would have died the wife of Thomas Culpepper.'

So ended the life of Henry's 5th Queen in 1542.

Children: None.

Katherine Parr

6th wife of Henry VIII

Born 1512

Died 1548

Buried Sudeley Castle, Gloucestershire

Henry's 6th and Last Wife

After the execution of Catherine Howard in 1542 for adultery and treason it was not long before Henry VIII was considering yet another wife.

He chose for his sixth partner Katherine Parr, daughter of Sir Thomas Parr and Maud, daughter of Sir Thomas Green. The Parr family came from Lancashire, where they held the Manor of Parr, near St Helens. Towards the end of the fourteenth century Sir William de Parre married Elizabeth, daughter and heiress of Baron Thomas de Roos of Kendal Castle.

Katherine Parr was born in 1512 at Kendal Castle. She learnt Latin, Greek and other languages. In 1523, before Katherine was twelve, negotiations were started for a marriage to Lord Scope's son, but this did not come to anything. A better offer came from England: Lord Borough of Gainsborough. He died and left Katherine a wealthy widow. She was then married to John Neville, Lord Latimer of Snape Hall, Yorkshire. He died in 1542 and Katherine was a widow once more.

Sir Thomas Seymour had eyes on Katherine and wanted to marry her, but once he discovered that the King was showing an interest he decided to step aside. On 12 July 1543, in a ceremony of great splendour, Henry and Katherine were married at Hampton Court.

Sometime during 1543 Katherine gave Henry a coat made of

Kendal cloth. Henry was so pleased he ordered another and one for his fool, Patche. Certainly other members of Henry's court ordered coats of this very high quality Kendal cloth and this stimulated commerce in the town where she was born.

Katherine was able to persuade Henry to restore to Mary and Elizabeth the title of princess. She took an interest in their education, recruiting tutors and theologians such as Hugh Latimer.

Stephen Gardiner, Bishop of Winchester, made accusations against Katherine to the King. The King listened and agreed to an investigation and then listed a bill of articles setting out her treacheries. She threw herself on his mercy and it seemed he was more than willing to forgive her. The charges were probably false in any case, and Henry perhaps knew it.

In 1544 Katherine, though not crowned Queen, was appointed Regent during Henry's absence in France.

The King was not getting any younger. He was having to be transported from place to place by litter and his ulcerated leg was causing more pain, and he was often having fevers.

On 28 January 1547 the King died. Katherine retired to Chelsea where once more she was courted by the still-ambitious Sir Thomas Seymour, then Baron Seymour of Sudeley, Lord High Admiral of England. It is said they were secretly married on 3 March 1547, only thirty-four days after the King's death. Even as late as May the marriage had still not been acknowledged but on 25 June young King Edward gave his consent.

It seems the approval was short-lived. Articles of impeachment against Sir Thomas state, 'You married the Queen so soon after the late King's death that if she had conceived straight after it should have been accounted a great doubt whether the child born should have been the late King's or yours, whereby a marvellous danger might have crushed to the quiet of the realm.' He was duly executed on Tower Hill on 20 March 1549.

A child was born at Sudeley Castle on 30 August 1548, a girl, christened Mary. Three days after the birth puerperal fever set in and Katherine became frequently delirious. She died on 7 September 1548. At her wish she was buried at Sudeley Castle. The service was conducted by Bishop Coverdale; the chief mourner was Lady Jane Grey.

It does not seem clear what happened to Katherine's daughter, Mary, but she possibly died young. Henry VIII's funeral took place at St George's Chapel, Windsor; he was laid to rest by his dear Jane Seymour. A space had been left for Katherine Parr to join him; that place was filled by King Charles I in 1649.

The death of Katherine, only eighteen months after Henry, ended a chapter of history. Henry, our most married king (six wives) was followed to the grave by Katherine, our most married Queen (four husbands).

Henry had seemed callous, unfeeling and some even say brutal but all that he had craved was a son and heir. He had divorced two wives, and executed two others. His son, Edward, did succeed his father, but was a sickly child who died aged sixteen, having ruled for only six years.

Children: No issue to Henry.

Lady Jane Grey

Born 1537

Died 1554

Buried Chapel of St Peter ad Vincula, Tower of London

Queen for Nine Days

Parliament had given Henry VIII a power that no monarch had previously had: that of being able to bequeath the Crown of England in his will.

In December 1546, Henry made his will, in which he said that the crown would go to Edward and his heirs, then Mary and her heir, then Elizabeth and her heir and then to the children of Francis Brandon.

When it was obvious that Edward VI was dying, the Duke of Northumberland made a determined effort to keep the royal power Protestant and not let it go to Mary Tudor. In May 1553 Lord Guildford of Dudley, son of the Duke of Northumberland, married Lady Jane Grey, daughter of Frances Brandon and Henry Grey, Duke of Suffolk.

The Duke of Northumberland was working on the possibility that if Henry VIII could leave the throne in his will, so Edward VI could do the same and cut out Mary Tudor and Elizabeth. The Duke persuaded the young Edward to make a will declaring Mary and Elizabeth illegitimate and declaring Lady Jane Grey as his successor. Edward died on 6 July 1553, but the news was suppressed until they had summoned the Lord Mayor and city dignitaries, and got their agreement to Lady Grey becoming Queen.

It seemed the stage was set for Northumberland to take over, but Mary had her supporters. The fleet deserted the Protestant cause and the Earl of Arundel succeeded in carrying out a coup d'état. The Lord Mayor now declared in favour of Mary.

The whole situation had changed. The Duke of Suffolk told his daughter, now imprisoned in the Tower, to take down her canopy – her reign was over. Those who had sought to take the throne were now in the tower as prisoners.

Both the Dukes of Suffolk and of Northumberland were executed in 1553. Lady Jane Grey and Lord Guildford of Dudley had to wait until the following year to know their fate.

In January 1554 Lord Guildford of Dudley said goodbye to his wife, but she said it was not advisable – she said that they would soon meet in a better place. Jane did agree to stand at the window and see him leave for the scaffold on Tower Hill. He was crying when he left and, still standing at the window, she saw his headless body brought back.

Later that day she came down the stairs from the Gentlemen Gaolers' lodgings wearing a black dress, the same one she had worn for her trial. She was very composed as she made her speech. Queen Mary Tudor had offered her pardon if she recanted and became Catholic. At the scaffold she gave her prayer book to the lieutenant and her handkerchief to her nurse. She approached the block blindfolded, saying, 'You will not take it off before I lay me down?' 'No, madam,' came the reply.

She knelt down, groping trying to find the block. 'Where is it?' she asked, but nobody moved forward to help. 'What shall I do? What shall I do?' she pleaded. Eventually a spectator came forward to help her. She bent down. 'Lord into thy hands I commit my spirit.'

So ended the life of this beautiful young lady because of the ambitions of her father-in-law and to a certain extent her father as well.

Mary Tudor or Mary I

Wife to Philip II of Spain
Born 1516
Died 1558
Buried Westminster Abbey

Bloody Mary

Mary Tudor was the only surviving child of Henry VIII and Catherine of Aragon and she was born on 18 February 1516 at Greenwich Palace. The Princess Catherine Plantagenet and the Duchess of Norfolk were her godmothers. She was placed in the care of the Countess of Salisbury, a devout Catholic.

On 28 February 1518, a son was born to Francis I and Cardinal Wolsey opened negotiations for a marriage between Mary and the newborn heir to the French throne. A bridal ceremony took place on 5 October 1518; eventually Mary would marry the dauphin when he was fourteen. Because of political problems with foreign policy, the agreement was called off. The Emperor Charles V and James IV were after Mary's hand, but neither would come to anything. Now Mary was ten years of age and three attempts had been made to marry her off. Thoughts of a marriage were dropped and more attention was paid to her education.

The divorce of Henry VIII and Catherine of Aragon, Mary's parents, reared its ugly head and Mary, who had been staying with her mother, was separated from her. They came together again for a few weeks and this was the last they were to see of each other. The divorce was finally made possible by breaking away from the Church in Rome and setting up the Catholic Church of England. Catherine of Aragon returned to Kimbolton Castle where she died on 7 January 1536.

At the end of 1535, when she knew she did not have much time to live, she requested that Mary might be able to visit, or maybe take up residence nearby, but both requests were refused and Mary was naturally bitterly disappointed. There was no love between Mary and the woman who took her mother's place as Queen – Anne Boleyn. The same year that Catherine of Aragon died, Anne Boleyn married Henry VIII and Elizabeth I was born. When Anne Boleyn was under threat of execution, she hoped for a reprieve by offering to look after Mary as her own daughter. This was refused.

It was Henry VIII's third wife, Jane Seymour, who secured reconciliation between Mary and her father. It was yet another bitter blow to Mary when Jane Seymour, who had befriended her, died giving birth to Edward VI. Mary was the chief mourner at Jane's funeral.

There was several more attempts to get Mary married into the French royal family, but when Henry VIII died in 1547, Mary was now thirty-one years of age and still unmarried. Mary assumed the throne in 1553 after the death of the sickly Edward VI.

She set about restoring the Catholic faith to which she had always adhered. Archbishop Cranmer and Bishops Latimer and Ridley were all burned at the stake in Oxford for signing the document which declared that Henry VIII and Catherine of Aragon were not married, a document that made Mary illegitimate.

On 1 October 1553, in a magnificent state occasion, the coronation took place. The queen wore a superb gown of crimson velvet and miniver fur. Both Princess Elizabeth and Anne of Cleves attended the ceremony. Mary had now made history. She was the first Queen Regnant in the history of England. Now she was Queen, a marriage became more important, in the hope of continuing the Catholic succession.

Finally, an agreement was reached for her to marry Philip II of Spain. Philip left Corunna for England in July of 1554, landing at Southampton on 20 July. On Wednesday, 25 July, the marriage was celebrated at Winchester Cathedral. On the conclusion of the ceremony, a herald proclaimed the titles as follows:

Philip and Mary by the Grace of God; King and Queen of England, France, Naples, Jerusalem and Ireland; Defender of the Faith; Princes of Spain and Sicily; Archdukes of Austria; Dukes of Milan; Burgundy and Brabant; Counts of Hapsburg, Flanders and Tyrol.

From the wedding ceremony, they went to Basing House, home of the Marquis of Winchester, then to Windsor Castle, where a series of festivities were held. During the celebrations, Philip was created Knight of the Garter. The festivities were then transferred to Richmond Palace and then the City of London and Whitehall, but were interrupted by the death of the Duke of Norfolk, for whom Mary called for court mourning. The King and Queen went to Hampton Court.

It was shortly after this that a period of persecution of the Protestants gained Mary the title 'Bloody Mary'. John Knox, the Scottish reformer and preacher, was openly calling her 'that wicked Jezebel of England'.

News was given out in 1555 that the Queen had given birth to a son, but the news was later declared false. There were also signs of Mary and Philip drifting apart. He found she had a very short temper. She in turn said he was making ungentlemanly advances to Margaret Dacre, one of the queen's attendants. Philip left England for a time on the pretence he had to visit his other estates.

By 1558, the Queen was becoming more depressed. Her illness was not improving. She was suffering from fever and dropsy. As things were getting progressively worse, she received extreme unction and had desired a Mass be celebrated in her room. At the elevation of the host she raised her eyes at the benediction and died. She was forty-two years of age and her death was probably due to a malignant growth.

She lay in state in the chapel of St James's Palace. On 14 December 1558, she was buried in Westminster Abbey.

Mary, who was a king's daughter, a king's sister and a king's wife, chose no great finery for her funeral, but a simple dress of a religious order.

She told Mrs Rise, a lady-in-waiting, that when they opened her up after death, they would find 'Calais' engraved on her heart.

This was a reference to the fact that during Mary's reign she lost Calais as a possession, the last English foothold in Europe.

Although Mary was buried in Westminster Abbey, her tomb was covered by a pile of rubble for forty-five years until the burial of her half-sister Elizabeth in 1603.

Children: None.

Elizabeth I

Born 1533

Died 1603

Buried Westminster Abbey

The Virgin Queen

On Sunday, 7 September 1533, Queen Anne Boleyn gave birth to a daughter at Greenwich Palace. Henry VIII tried not to show his disappointment at another daughter – it seemed God was still punishing him. However, that child, christened Elizabeth, would become one of England's greatest queens.

She spent her early years at Hatfield with Mary, her half-sister, as a Maid of Honour to look after her. This was not to Mary's liking and she refused to call Elizabeth 'Princess'. So began the conflict between the sisters which continued until Mary's death in 1558.

Elizabeth's mother, Anne Boleyn, was executed in 1536 and both Elizabeth and Mary had the title 'Princess' taken from them. Without the title of Princess, the worth of these little girls in the marriage stakes had been devalued. As far as Elizabeth was concerned, the question of marriage had arisen in 1535 when she was but two years of age. The Duc d'Angoulême, younger son of Francis I, had been suggested, but the offer was not taken seriously at the English court.

It was not until Katherine Parr became Henry VIII's wife that Mary and Elizabeth were taken to live in the royal palace and received a formal education. Elizabeth was a bright child and learnt quickly.

Henry VIII died in 1547 and his son, Edward, became king. Elizabeth stayed with Katherine Parr and met Thomas Seymour, who married Katherine Parr. He began to flirt with Elizabeth, who was only just fourteen years of age. He snatched risks; there was horseplay; he would sneak into her bedroom and tickle her and smack her bottom. Katherine Parr, who was now expecting his child, thought his attention to Elizabeth would have to stop. She sent Elizabeth off to Cheshunt to the home of Sir Anthony Denny.

Edward VI's reign was short. He died of consumption on 6 July 1553. Lady Jane Grey became unofficially the queen for nine days and was arrested and executed in 1554. Mary Tudor succeeded her half-brother Edward, but her reign was also to be short. She died in 1558 having married Philip of Spain but produced no children.

Elizabeth, at Hatfield Palace, was waiting for a call to succeed her sister. The call came in 1558 while she was sitting under a tree, reading. Elizabeth was not twenty-five years of age and as a queen her marriage would be of interest to many, particularly to the royal houses of Europe.

In the following years, callers in the form of ambassadors or courtiers came and went, but nothing materialised. Ten years later, she was ill with smallpox. She recovered and four years on she had a fever, probably colic, and it was thought by her courtiers that she would die. However, she recovered. This once more raised the possibility of marriage.

The Earl of Leicester, who sat by her bed while she was ill, was considered. There was, however, a stumbling block. Robert Dudley, Earl of Leicester, was already married to Amy Robsart. There was a turn of events when Amy Robsart was found dead at the bottom of the stairs of Cumnor House. Questions were raised at the time about whether she fell down the stairs or whether she was pushed. One thing was certain, that if Elizabeth had had any serious thoughts about marrying Robert Dudley then they ended with Amy Robsart's death because of the scandal that might surround Elizabeth as a possible accomplice.

Just a few years later, she was to be faced with another major problem – that of Mary, Queen of Scots. Pressure was being brought to bear that the Scottish queen, seeking sanctuary in England, should be executed. She was a threat to the throne, said some. Ambassadors from Scotland and France came to Elizabeth pleading and threatening invasion if she harmed a hair on Mary's head. Finally a death warrant was signed. History, at this point, is not absolutely clear as to whether Elizabeth signed the death warrant as a protection of the realm, so that in case of Elizabeth's sudden death, Mary could be executed and prevented from becoming Queen; or whether it was Elizabeth's intention to end this sad episode by an immediate execution. The signed document was sent, probably by Secretary Davidson, to Fotheringay Castle where Mary was being held. Mary's gaoler, Sir Thomas Bromley, saw the Queen's signature and so the execution was duly carried out on 8 February 1587.

When Elizabeth learnt that the sentence had been carried out, she was more than extremely angry. Secretary Davidson was sent to the Tower and her faithful servant, Lord Burleigh, kept away from the Queen in case he too would be sent to the Tower. Secretary Davidson was later released, but never held another office of the crown.

Sir Thomas Bromley, who had the execution carried out, is said to have died of a broken heart within a year. James VI of Scotland, Mary, Queen of Scots' son, could not or would not invade England in reprisal for his mother's death as there was every indication he would eventually succeed Elizabeth I.

Only one year after Mary, Queen of Scots' death, Philip II of Spain had sent his great Armada against England and Elizabeth went to Tilbury to review her troops, who were guarding the Thames approaches. She there made a very historic speech and the following is perhaps the best-remembered extract:

I know I have but the body of a weak and feeble woman; but I have the heart and stomach of a king; and a king of England too!

The battle went in England's favour and the Spanish fleet was routed.

Elizabeth's reign was not without other disappointments. Robert Dudley, Earl of Leicester, died and she missed him at court. Another of her favourites, Sir Walter Raleigh, was imprisoned for not only, as she said, seducing Bess Throckmorton, one of the queen's Maids of Honour, but because all this had been done behind the Queen's back, including concealing the fact they were married and she had given birth to a child. Another of her favourites, Robert Devereux, Earl of Essex, who had been sent to Ireland by the Queen, had deserted his post and returned to England. He was arrested and confined in York Place. After a trial, he was executed in 1601 at the Tower of London.

Elizabeth was now, by normal standards, old. She was sixty-eight and in 1603, on her way to her seventieth birthday, she died at three o'clock in the morning on 27 May. Her body was conveyed from Richmond to Whitehall by river, where it had lain for five weeks, watched over continuously by her ladies-in-waiting.

The state funeral took place in Westminster Abbey with an effigy of the queen on top of the coffin, fully robed, wearing her crown and carrying an orb and sceptre. It was so like her that it brought gasps and tears from the Londoners who came to see the Queen's last journey.

She was the first English monarch to give her name to an age and she was the last of the Tudors. It was a reign of almost forty-five years, which brought many changes. It brought glory and prosperity to the country. The Elizabethan Age had entered the history book.

Children: None.

Historical Background: The Stuarts

James VI of Scotland became James I of England in 1603. The following year the Hampton Court Conference decided on changes to the Book of Common Prayer, resulting in the Authorised Version of the Bible or the 'King James Bible'.

In 1605 there was the Gunpowder Plot to blow up Parliament and the King. It failed and Guy Fawkes and other conspirators were executed. By 1620 the Pilgrim Fathers had set off for the New World. James died in 1625 and was succeeded by his second son, Charles I. This was a troubled reign, in which the King wanted overall rule, but Parliament said no. It eventually led to civil war, which set Englishman against Englishman and brother against brother. The conflict would last six years and end in Charles I's arrest, trial and execution on 30 January 1648 in Whitehall. Our smallest king was also the only king to be executed.

Oliver Cromwell was proclaimed Lord Protector and re-mained so until he died in 1658. It took the rest of that year and all the following to arrange for the Restoration of the Monarchy and the return of Charles II as King.

In his twenty-five-year rule, he had the problems of the Great Plague in 1665 and the Great Fire of 1666. There were the Dutch Wars of 1672–1674, plots to assassinate the King, and his thirteen mistresses to contend with.

Charles II died in 1685 without a legitimate heir. His brother succeeded as James II for what was to be a short two-and-a-half-year reign. His downfall was through trying to restore the Roman Catholic religion. So James was deposed in favour of his daughter Mary, who was married to William of Orange. So for the first time in our history, we had a joint rulership with a Queen Regnant, Mary II, and a King Regnant, William III.

In 1692 came the Massacre of Glencoe because the MacDonalds of Glencoe refused to take the oath of allegiance. They were massacred by the Campbells, their hereditary enemies. In 1689, in Ireland, the Roman Catholics rose in support of the deposed James II and by 1690, after the Battle of the Boyne, James II fled to France into exile.

Queen Mary II died in 1694 and William ruled alone until his death in 1702. There were no children, so Mary's sister Anne, also a daughter of James II, assumed the throne in 1702.

During Anne's reign, the Duke of Marlborough, John Churchill, was winning glorious battles against the French at Blenheim, Ramillies, Oudenarde and in Spain at Barcelona, Almeira, Saragossa.

Anne married her cousin Prince George of Denmark, had seventeen children and all died young. She died in 1714 and so ended the 111-year reign of the Stuarts.

Anne of Denmark

Wife of James I
Born 1574
Died 1619
Buried Westminster Abbey

The Queen Who Gave Us Two Princes of Wales

The death of Elizabeth I in 1603 was the end of the reign of the Tudors. James, the son of Mary Queen of Scots and Lord Darnley, became James I of England and Scotland (VI). James was born on 19 June 1566 in Edinburgh Castle. James was separated from his mother in 1567 and was never to see her again. He was raised by the Earl of Mar and was proclaimed King of Scotland on his mother's abdication.

When James began to look for a wife, he applied himself with diligence and energy to the task. He finally met Anne, the fourteen-year-old daughter of the King of Denmark. Anne was typically Scandinavian in her beauty, tall and slender with golden hair. The wedding took place almost immediately at Christiania. They arrived in Scotland on 15 May 1590 and the Queen's coronation was arranged with utmost speed and was held on 25 July 1603.

There were to be several children from this marriage. Henry, the eldest, became Prince of Wales; then there were Elizabeth and Margaret, followed by Charles, who became Charles I and succeeded his father. Then there were Robert, Mary and Sophia. Only three of these would grow to adulthood.

Sophia died after only three days and is buried in Innocent's Corner at Westminster Abbey in a very touching cradle-shaped tomb. Her sister Princess Mary died in 1607 aged two and lies next to Sophia. Mary is shown reclining on her elbow on a cushion.

Queen Anne, it is said, had niceness of character and was royally gracious, but there was a lack of brains. She enjoyed the pleasures of life, but she did interest herself in other things such as the education of her children and she encouraged and was patron to Inigo Jones in his pursuits of the new Palladian style of architecture.

Eventually, Inigo Jones became Surveyor to the Crown. He built as part of the royal palace of Whitehall the Banqueting House, and he began the Queen's House at Greenwich for Anne, but she did not see its completion.

James's son Henry looked like his mother, but with a touch of the good looks of his grandfather, Lord Darnley. Henry possessed a charming smile and seemed to be able to grasp at an early age the art of being royal as a future king. Henry tragically died young in 1612 at the age of eighteen of a fever. His brother Charles would now be heir to the throne.

Elizabeth, their eldest daughter, was to marry the Elector Palatine of Hanover and from her line came the first of the Hanoverian kings of England.

The King and Queen seemed to follow different lives; and James seemed to prefer the company of men, and in particular was infatuated by George Villiers. This handsome youth certainly had a rapid rise at court: knighted in 1615, Earl of Buckingham in 1617, Marquis in 1619 and finally a Duke in 1623. George Villiers had a combination of strength and beauty with dark eyes and chestnut hair and James accepted him like a son with strong physical attachments as shown by their letters to each other.

Anne, for her part, enjoyed the masques and balls at court. She did not share either bed or palace with the King for ten years.

Anne died on 2 March 1619 aged forty-five. The King saw no reason why he should visit her on her deathbed, nor even attend the funeral. Anne was laid to rest in Westminster Abbey. Anne had come from Denmark to be consort to the King and not only bring about the new dynasty of the Stuarts but also the uniting of England and Scotland and she had done her part in continuing the royal line by producing two Princes of Wales. The chief mourner, who must always be a woman at a queen's funeral, was the Countess of Arundel.

Children	*Born*	*Died*
Henry	1594	1612
Stillborn child	1595	
Elizabeth	1596	1662
Margaret	1598	1600
Charles (I)	1600	1649
Robert Bruce	1602	1602
Stillborn child	1603	
Mary	1605	1607
Sophia	1607	1607

Anne of Denmark also had three miscarriages.

Henrietta Maria

Wife of Charles I
Born 1609
Died 1699
Buried Cathedral of St Denis, Paris

'The Sweetest Creature in France'

Charles I, second son of James I and Anne of Denmark, decided to look at marriage possibilities while Prince of Wales. He travelled with the Marquess of Buckingham incognito to see the young Infanta of Spain. They called themselves Jack and Tom Smith. Charles was convinced he loved the Spanish princess. There were complications, however. The King of Spain did not want his daughter to marry a heretic. So the King wrote to Rome asking the Pope not to agree to such a marriage. Charles sent another rider off to Rome asking the Pope to agree. The Pope agreed with Charles; he could see no reason to prevent the marriage. In fact he thought it might help the Catholics in England to have a Catholic Queen.

There were strings attached, however, by both the Pope and the Spanish King. They brought forward new proposals. By the time Charles eventually left Spain he was more in favour of war than marriage. So the marriage to the Infanta of Spain did not take place.

Charles now turned his sights on France and Henrietta Maria, sister of King Louis XIII. Negotiations proceeded fairly quickly and an agreement was reached that the marriage should take place provided the English Catholics received the same concessions as those granted in the Spanish marriage terms. In May of 1625 a final agreement was reached and a marriage by proxy took place at

Notre-Dame in Paris. Charles described his bride as 'the sweetest creature in France'. Within a month the fourteen-year-old Henrietta Maria, still only a child, set sail from Boulogne to Dover and Charles watched her arrival from Dover Castle. She was a petite little figure, which would suit Charles, England's smallest king, who was less than 5 ft.

On her arrival Henrietta Maria had a speech all prepared but forgot her words and began to cry; but Charles said she was not among strangers. Then Charles glanced at her feet to see if she was wearing high-heeled shoes. 'Sire,' she said, 'I stand on mine own two feet. I have no help by art. This high am I, neither higher or lower.'

Henrietta never became Princess of Wales, – just missing that title by a few months because of the death of James I, she became Queen Consort instead.

On 12 June 1625 a second marriage ceremony took place at Canterbury Cathedral. Four years later their first child was born but died after only hours. When the doctors came to ask the King whether they should save the mother or child, the King's reply was, 'I would rather the cast was taken than we should lose the mould.'

Twelve months later the future Charles II was born in May of 1630. He was baptised on 27 June 1630 with all the royal splendour of such an occasion: taffeta and damask clothes, carpets, two organs and the presence of heralds, ambassadors and representatives of the City of London. Madame Peronne, who looked after the Queen during her pregnancy, attended.

Charles and Henrietta Maria were to have eight children. After Charles in 1630 came Mary, who married William II of Holland. Then James, Elizabeth, Anne, Catherine, Henry and Henrietta.

Charles and Henrietta were happy together. She had matured over the previous few years. While Rubens and Van Dyck painted for the King, Inigo Jones designed scenery and costumes for the court masques. Cromwell was emerging as a formidable figure in Parliament.

However, the couple's happy times were not to last long. The King and Parliament could not agree about the Divine Right of the King and rule of Parliament. From these problems, and the King bursting into parliament to arrest five members, came the outbreak of the Civil War in 1642. The war continued for six years, and even with the help of the King's nephew, Prince Rupert of the Rhine, the final battle at Naseby was lost. The King prepared to fight to the end but Prince Rupert took his horse's reins and led him away from the battle. The King's cause was lost and being a Stuart he decided to surrender himself to the Scots; but eventually they sold him back to Cromwell.

A trial took place at Westminster Hall and finally the King was sentenced to death in 1648. The execution took place outside the Banqueting House of Whitehall Palace on 30 January 1649.

Charles could well have been restored as King if he had agreed to the terms of Parliament, but Charles believed in the Divine Right of the King and died a martyr for his cause.

Henrietta Maria went to France, where Charles, Prince of Wales and Prince James joined her after they had been at the King's side in battle.

Henrietta Maria had not been crowned Queen as she was Roman Catholic. She was to live a further twenty years after Charles's execution and died in 1669.

Children	Born	Died
Charles	1629	same day
Charles (II)	1630	1685
Mary	1631	1660
James (II)	1633	1701
Elizabeth	1635	1650
Anne	1637	1640 (died aged 3 of consumption)
Catherine	1639	same day
Henry	1640	1660
Henrietta	1644	1670

Catherine of Braganza

Wife of Charles II
Born 1638
Died 1705
Buried Belem, Lisbon

Wife of the Merry Monarch

With the tragedy of the Civil War over and the nine-year rule of Cromwell's protectorate ended with his death in 1658, the country was now ready to call back the monarchy from exile. The throne was offered to Charles, Prince of Wales, who accepted and became Charles II in 1660. After his coronation, Charles turned his thoughts to finding a wife. There was a long list of candidates to be considered and most of these were dismissed very quickly for one reason or another.

When Charles set his eyes on Princess Catherine (daughter of John IV Duke of Braganza and Louise Maria, daughter of the 8th Duke of Medina Sidonia) it was through a portrait of her with which he was very pleased. 'That person cannot be unhandsome,' he said. Perhaps what swayed his decision was her dowry of £300,000 in cash plus the ports of Tangiers and Bombay and other trading rights in the new world.

On 21 May 1662, they were married by the Bishop of London at one ceremony and privately according to the Catholic religion at the Queen's request. Charles II had a very colourful court and must have been very bewildered to see Catherine with her strict convent upbringing. She arrived with her own ladies-in-waiting and a retinue of monks.

The King and Queen moved into Hampton Court Palace and the King presented her with a list of ladies-in-waiting who would look after her. The list of names included Lady Castlemaine. The Queen immediately crossed her name off. Charles was furious, and insisted she remained. A quarrel followed and Charles dismissed all the Portuguese ladies and sent them home. The Queen was now an isolated figure speaking only a little English, with no close friends, and she became quite miserable.

Catherine then decided to relent and allow Lady Castlemaine to remain and decided on new tactics. She befriended Lady Castlemaine and began competing with her for the King's affection. It worked, for the King responded and religiously returned to the palace each night. Then the Queen fell ill and Charles spent many hours by her side. She recovered and the King was happy once more.

Frances Stuart – 'La Belle Stuart' as she was referred to – arrived at the court and it was not long before the King was paying more than casual attention to her. She refused to surrender herself to the King. Some of the King's close friends set up a committee and took the title 'The Committee for the Getting of Mistress Stuart for the King'.

A banquet was held and during the evening they would try to get Mistress Stuart intoxicated and then perhaps she would go to bed with the King. This plan had to be chopped when the Queen unexpectedly arrived at the banquet. Eventually Frances Stuart became Frances, Duchess of Richmond and she was the model for Britannia on the British coinage.

On to the royal scene came Mistress Nell Gwynne and another, Moll Davies. Mistresses came and went but Nell Gwynne remained a favourite till Charles died. Apart from being an actress, Nell had wit and charm. The King allowed her a house in Pall Mall and £4,000 a year. She gave birth to a son to Charles and he was created Duke of St Albans.

In May of 1670 Charles's sister Minette (Henrietta) arrived from France. One of her ladies-in-waiting was Louise de Kéroualle, and Charles liked her, so she too became a mistress and later she was created Duchess of Portsmouth. She was to give birth to the tenth and the last illegitimate child to Charles from any of his thirteen mistresses.

During February 1685 the King was ill; Charles knew he was

dying. He even joked to his mistresses around his bed, and the court officials who had to be in attendance, 'I am sorry, gentlemen, for being such a long time a-dying.' He told his brother, James, Duke of York, who was to succeed him, to look after Louise and his children. 'And let not poor Nellie starve.' And the King passed away.

Catherine of Braganza returned to Portugal and lived a further twenty-one years. For a time she was Queen Regent of Portugal when her brother King Pedro died.

Barbara, Lady Castlemaine went to France and so too did Louise, Duchess of Portsmouth, where she lived for almost another fifty years. Nell Gwynne died two years after the King.

Queen Catherine of Braganza, who had married Charles and come to live in a foreign country without friends or staff, and had to live with the comings and going of the mistresses of the King, had not been able to produce an heir to the throne.

Catherine died in 1705 of an attack of colic and was buried at Belem.

Children of Catherine of Braganza

Miscarriage	1662
Stillborn child	1666
Stillborn child	1668
Stillborn child	1669

Charles II's mistresses' children

Lucy Walter	A son, James Duke of Monmouth
Elizabeth, Lady Shannon	A daughter, Charlotte Fitzroy
Katherine	A son, Charles Fitzcharles, Duke of Leeds
	A daughter, Katherine, became a nun
	A daughter who died young

Barbara, Duchess of Cleveland	A daughter, Anne Fitzroy
(Lady Castlemaine)	A son, Charles Fitzroy, Duke of Southampton
	A son, Henry Fitzroy, Duke of Grafton
	A daughter, Charlotte Fitzroy
	A son, George Fitzroy, Duke of Northumberland
	A daughter, Barbara, became a nun
	A son, Charles Beauclerk, Duke of St Albans
	A son, James Beauclerk
Louise, Duchess of Portsmouth	A son, Charles Lennox, Duke of Richmond
Mary 'Moll' Davis	A daughter, Mary Tudor

Anne Hyde

1st wife of James II
Born 1637
Died 1671
Buried Westminster Abbey

Anne the Commoner

James II was the second son of Charles I and Henrietta Maria. James was born in 1633 and was considered to be a beautiful blue-eyed baby with fair hair and was his mother's favourite. For the first fifty-two years of his life he would have to be content with being just Prince James, brother of Charles, Prince of Wales. Charles was the eldest, born 1630 followed by Mary in 1631 and then James in 1633.

James was just nine years of age when the Civil War broke out and he spent most of the war at Oxford. At the end of the war his father was executed and James was in exile until the Restoration of the Monarchy. He was now twenty-six years of age.

In 1656 James had met Anne Hyde at the court at St Germain. She was a lady-in-waiting and instantly James took a liking to her. A contract of marriage was eventually signed in 1659. There were those of the King's advisers who said he could not, should not, marry a commoner and some even referred to Anne as a whore. Anne proved an equal match for the conspirators and she was certainly in full command of her life. Even Anne Hyde's father, the Earl of Clevedon, was opposed to the match. It was James's brother, King Charles II, who finally made James's mind up for him by ordering him to marry the girl and honour his contract. The marriage finally took place in secret on 3 September. It was a happy marriage and her characteristics of being powerful and also very intelligent were certainly of help to the future King.

Anne was to give birth to seven children, including: Mary, who would eventually marry William of Orange; Charles, Duke of Cambridge, who died young of smallpox; and Anne, who was born 1665 and was later to marry Prince George of Denmark.

James was something of a womaniser and fell in love with Arabella Churchill. He had a long and lasting affair with her. Arabella's brother was John, who became Duke of Malborough.

James, assisted by his wife Anne and by some members of the court, travelled to France and was converted to the Catholic faith.

In March 1671 his wife Anne died of cancer after a long illness. Although this had been a happy marriage James did not mourn for too long. Anne was buried in the Stuart vault of the Mary Queen of Scots Chapel in Westminster Abbey.

Children	Born	Died
Charles	1660	1661
Mary (II)	1162	1694
James	1663	1669
Anne	1665	1714
Edgar	1667	1671
Henrietta	1669	1669
Katherine	1671	1671

Mary of Modena

2nd wife of James II

Born 1658

Died 1718

Buried Chaillot

Charles and Catherine of Braganza had no children. It was becoming obvious that one day James would become King, but he had no sons to succeed him. Finding another wife seemed to be of some urgency. Lord Peterborough was sent to the European courts to look for a possible princess. It seemed that James was fussy, as some were deemed too fat or too ugly and one even had red hair, which James detested. Finally Princess Mary of Modena in Italy, who was about to enter a convent, was told she was about to marry James, Duke of York. Mary sobbed and screamed for two days; she was but seventeen years of age and he was forty, living in a country she had not seen and only heard about.

On 21 November 1673 Princess Mary of Modena arrived at Dover, and they were wedded and bedded the same day. Mary was tall and dark and she became a very loyal wife to James despite the original misgivings. This was not considered an ideal match for the country as a whole because James and his new wife were both Catholic. This marriage certainly contributed to the downfall of James as King James II. There were plots and counterplots and even a plot to kill King Charles II and place his brother James on the throne.

It was in 1685 that Charles II died and James became James II. It seems odd that in 1681 there were those who wanted James excluded from the throne, yet those same people now welcomed him as the new king. They would turn again and rejoice at James's deposition in 1688.

James was now fifty-one years of age and his wife was still trying desperately to have a child. In fact she had six pregnancies, of which two were miscarriages. Three other babies died in their first year and another died at the age of four.

The Queen was once more pregnant after a lapse of five years. Everyone was convinced that this time it would be a healthy boy. During the Queen's agony in labour pains there were at least thirty onlookers in the small bedroom at St James's Palace. Despite all the witnesses, the newborn was carried into another room without the witnesses first seeing the child. A rumour then spread that the child was a girl and had been changed in the other room for a boy born to a miller's wife. Whatever took place will never be known, but the child was christened James Francis Edward Stuart (later to be known as the Old Pretender).

King James's reign was to be brief as after only two years he was deposed. Everything seemed to be against him. His daughter Mary was married to the ambitious William of Orange. Anne, her sister, suggested her claim to the throne, as did John Churchill, Duke of Malborough and his wife Sarah. The Church was against him and his queen because of their persecution of the Protestants. On 21 December 1688 the King sent Queen Mary and his son to France and himself left England shortly afterwards. As if in a final gesture of defiance he threw the Great Seal of England into the Thames.

James took refuge in France, joining his wife and son at St Germain. While in exile in 1692 Mary gave birth to a daughter named Louise Mary and nicknamed Solace.

Mary spent her years in exile planning ways to restore James to the throne of England and so see her son James Francis take his rightful place. James II suffered a heart attack in 1701 and died three weeks later. Mary attempted to help her son after the 1715 rebellion to regain the throne, but it was to be fruitless, as was the 1745 rebellion by her grandson Charles, 'Bonnie Prince Charlie'.

The Queen died in 1718 after thirty years in exile and is buried with her husband at St Germain in Calais. She was buried first at Chaillot but when the convent was suppressed evidence of her burial disappeared.

Children	Born	Died
Stillborn child		1674
Katherine	1675	1675
Stillborn child		1675
Isabella	1676	1681
Charles	1677	1677
Elizabeth	1678	1678
Stillborn child		1681
Charlotte Maria	1682	1682
Stillborn child		1683
Stillborn child		1684
James Francis[1]	1688	1766
Louise	1692	1712

[1] From James Francis, Charles Edward Louis John ('Bonnie Prince Charlie') was born in 1720. He died 30 January 1788 in Rome and was buried in Frascati Cathedral but his remains were later moved to St Peter's Basilica in the Vatican.

Mary II

Wife of William of Orange, William III
Born 1662
Died 1694
Buried Westminster Abbey

Dear Lemon

Mary was the eldest daughter of James, Duke of York and his first wife, Anne Hyde. She was born at St James's Palace on 30 April 1662. Her early years were spent at the home of Clarendon, her grandfather at Twickenham, and later she moved to Richmond Palace under the care of Lady Frances Villiers. Among the children she played with was Sarah Jennings (later the Duchess of Marlborough). The two sisters, Mary and her younger sister Anne (later Queen Anne), were instructed in religion by the Bishop of London (Compton) and they were both well versed in the Protestant religion.

Because of the death of her brother Edgar, Duke of Cambridge, in 1671, she became heiress presumptive and a wedding match became important. The possible match between Mary and William of Orange was not at first agreed to; in fact, it was discussed in 1672 but not finally agreed to until 1677. Mary was now fifteen years of age and William was thirty-two. When Mary was told the wedding was agreed she wept for almost two days.

The marriage was solemnised by Bishop Compton in Mary's apartments on 4 November 1677. William and Mary returned to Holland to live near The Hague – William, however, seemed to treat her with coolness to the extent he never dined with her.

In 1688 the call came from England that Mary was required to accede to the throne after her father had been deposed. William, on the other hand, knew if he accompanied her to England he would be accepted only as a Prince Consort. On 13 February 1689 they sat side by side in the Banqueting House, Whitehall, where they were proclaimed joint rulers. William had made the journey to England in 1688 saying that Mary would come only if he were made King. This was the first and only time England had a joint rulership.

The coronation took place on 11 April 1689 in Westminster Abbey. Because a King and Queen were being crowned with equal status, a second coronation chair had to be made, which Westminster Abbey still possesses.

The couple's official residence was Whitehall Palace, which the King did not like as it was too damp and that affected his asthma. They moved to Hampton Court and found the rooms too small, so they asked Sir Christopher Wren to pull down the Tudor Palace and build a new Renaissance palace suitable for joint rulers. They moved to Holland House and finally bought Nottingham House in Kensington, asking Wren to enlarge the building. He made it into a typical E-shaped building called Kensington House, later to become Kensington Palace.

During William's absence in Holland, Mary amused herself at the palace of Whitehall with her ladies, playing Comet or Basset, and had dancing at the court. Unfortunately the large rambling palace at Whitehall with its tiltyard, bowling green and 2,000 rooms was destroyed by fire in 1698, except for the Banqueting House and the Henry VIII wine cellars.

In 1694 Mary was taken ill on 20 December though it was thought not of importance. On 23 December a rash broke out which was thought to be measles, but by Christmas Day it was agreed by her physician she was suffering from smallpox. William's parents had also died of the disease. Princess Anne, her sister, wanted to see her and was naturally refused. William was shedding tears and cried out that there was 'not hope for the queen', and from being the happiest he was going to be the miserablest creature upon earth. Late on 27 December she said goodbye to William and died half an hour later on 28 December 1694.

Her body was embalmed and lay in state at Whitehall until 5 March when a magnificent funeral costing over £50,000 was held. William III, in mourning for the death of his Queen, and according to custom did not attend.

Mary had lived her whole life in a continual dilemma. She was childless, she was also brotherless and after a quarrel with her sister Anne was virtually sisterless. Her father, James II, had been deposed as King and was now in exile in France, so she was effectively fatherless. As William for the most part chose to ignore her, she was also husbandless.

'Dear Lemon' was an endearing term of affection used by the Duchess of York, her stepmother, who wrote to her frequently and they got on well together. Mary was amiable, cheerful, well informed and could write easily in French and English and to a certain extent Dutch. She loved working and at Hampton Court there is still evidence of her horticultural interest.

William ruled alone for a further eight years but on 21 February 1702 he was thrown by his horse while riding at Hampton Court. He broke his collarbone but complications set in and he died on 8 March. William was buried quietly around midnight and not given a state funeral.

So ended a joint rulership – the first and last!

Children	Born
Stillborn child	1678
Stillborn child	1678
Stillborn child	1680

Anne

Wife of Prince George of Denmark
Born 1665
Died 1714
Buried Westminster Abbey

Brandy Nan

Anne was the third child born to James II and Anne Hyde. The male child Anne was carrying when she married James Duke of York died within six months. Mary would eventually become Queen Mary II. The Royal Family moved to Hampton Court and to Salisbury to avoid the plague which was ravishing London in 1665 when Anne was born. There were other children born to James and Anne but they all died young.

Anne was sent to her aunt Minette, the Duchess of Orleans, but a year later Minette died and Anne was sent back to England. In 1671 Anne Hyde died and Anne and her sister Mary were placed in the care of Lady Frances Villiers and went to live in Richmond Palace. They were there for nearly three years.

In 1683 Anne was informed that a marriage had been arranged for her with Prince George of Denmark, the younger brother of the Danish King. George was thirty and Anne eighteen. Prince George was described as good-looking, of large build with blond hair, and having a pleasant personality. The marriage took place on St Anne's Day, 28 July 1683 at St James's Palace, performed by Henry Compton, Bishop of London.

George was an affectionate husband to Anne and they began their married life at the Cockpit, Whitehall. This modest home, a gift of King Charles II, stood near to the present Downing Street. One of Anne's first duties in her new home was appoint Sarah

Jennings as her first Lady of the Bedchamber. This friendship would last for twenty years. In their correspondence to each other they adopted pseudonyms of Mrs Freeman (Sarah) and Mrs Morley (Anne).

In 1684 Anne's first child was a miscarriage and now Anne's extremely sad story of one death after another was to begin. She had seventeen children, all of them to die before their 11th birthday, except one. William, Duke of Gloucester did reach eleven in July 1700 and during his birthday celebrations he caught a chill and developed a sore throat. The physician who came to see William decided they should bleed him in order to get the fever down. William got worse and lived just four more days. Anne was with him when he died; she could not cry. She was stunned with grief. Anne was not yet Queen, but what could she offer the country as a future heir? It was decided by Parliament, with Anne's agreement, that if Anne produced no further children the crown would pass to the Protestant descendant of James I from Elizabeth, his daughter, who had married into the House of Hanover.

Anne's sister Mary had become Queen Mary II after the deposition of their father, James II. Mary was to be Queen for only five short years and William, her husband, continued until 1702 when he died and Anne became Queen.

The coronation was arranged for St George's Day, 23 April. Anne wore a gown of crimson velvet with a gold underobe and she was enriched with diamonds and rubies about her neck. Regardless of all this finery Anne was suffering from gout to such an extent she had the distinction of being the only monarch to be carried to their coronation.

Sarah Jennings and her husband John Churchill were now Duke and Duchess of Marlborough. Over the years Anne had bestowed titles and gifts on the couple but things were beginning to turn sour between Anne and Sarah. In 1708 Anne was struck another blow. Her husband, Prince George, who had been ill for some months, died on 28 October with Anne at his side. Now she had lost her father, mother, brother, sister, brother-in-law and all of her seventeen children. She was about to lose her lifelong companion Sarah. There were many arguments between them and it seemed Sarah was overstepping her authority. The friendship ended with Sarah's banishment from court.

Anne was to be queen until 1714. When she was getting to-wards the end of her twelve-year reign, and doctors were desperately trying to find a remedy for her illness. She was bled and they applied hot irons to blister the skin. She was given medicine to make her vomit, and her feet were covered in garlic and finally her head was shaved bare. She had to suffer all these indignities in the presence of seven doctors, her ladies-in-waiting and three members of the clergy.

She passed away on Sunday, 1 August 1714 and Dr John Arbuthnot wrote, 'Sleep was never more welcome to a weary traveller than death was to her.'

During Anne's reign, the Act of Union was signed in 1707, by which officially Scotland and England were joined. Anne was buried in Westminster Abbey.

Children	Born	Died
Stillborn child	1684	
Mary	1685	1687
Anne Sophia	1686	1687
Stillborn child		1687
Stillborn son		1687
Stillborn child		1688
William Henry	1689	1700
Mary	1690	1690 (same day)
George	1692	1692 (same day)
Stillborn child		1693
Stillborn child		1694
Stillborn child		1695
Stillborn child		1696
Stillborn twins		1697
Stillborn son		1697
Charles	1698	
Stillborn child		1700

Historical Background: The House of Hanover

On the death of Queen Anne without an heir the country reverted to the first Stuart King, James I, whose daughter Elizabeth had married the Palatine of Hanover and whose daughter Sophia in turn married the Elector of Hanover; their son George was the next Protestant in line.

George I had been King of England little over a year when James II's son, James Francis Stuart, the 'Old Pretender', attempted to regain the throne in 1715 in the Jacobite Rebellion. In this period Robert Walpole became the first man to be called Prime Minister. When George I, who spoke no English, died in 1727 his son, another George, became George II. He would be the last King to lead his army into war, at the Battle of Dettingen against the French. In 1745 came the Jacobite Rebellion by Bonnie Prince Charlie, son of the 'Old Pretender'. There was also war in Europe, the Battles of Minden, Lagos and Quiberon Bay; General Wolfe was fighting at the Heights of Abraham near Quebec and both he and the opposing French general, the Marquis de Montcalm, died. John Wesley began his great Methodist religious revival. George II died in 1760 and the throne went to his grandson, George III, as Frederick, Prince of Wales had died before his father.

George III, England's longest-reigning male monarch was king for sixty years. He, like the other Georges, had trouble with wars. The end of the Seven Years War came in 1763. There was tension with the American Colonies over the Stamp Act and then the tea tax, which culminated in the Boston Tea Party when men dressed as Red Indians dumped the tea in Boston Harbour. America was lost in the War of Independence.

During this period England was alone. France, Spain, Russia, Sweden and Denmark were all fighting Britain.

Then there came the French Revolution in 1789. The Battle of Trafalgar was a victory for Nelson and Britain against the French in 1805. Wellington was victorious against Napoleon at the Battle of Waterloo in 1815. In 1807 came the abolition of the slave trade.

The King in his declining years was suffering bouts of melancholy and his son George, Prince of Wales, was appointed Regent. On the death of George III in 1820 George, Prince Regent became George IV; it was a short reign of ten years. This period saw the introduction of tarmacadam roads, the arrival of the omnibus in 1829 and the police force the same year, although there was already a form of police force called the Bow Street Runners.

George IV's daughter, Charlotte, died in childbirth; so did the child. So the throne was now destined for George's brother, William, Duke of Clarence. This reign of William IV was even shorter, only seven years. This period saw the railways arrive in London 1836. New London Bridge by Sir John Rennie was opened. William IV and Queen Adelaide had an heir, so the throne was now destined for the Victorian era, when Alexandrina Victoria became Queen Victoria.

Sophia Dorothea of Celle

Wife of George I
Born 1666
Died 1726
Buried Celle Church, Hanover

The Tragic Love Story

The theme of the tragic love story of Sophia Dorothea and Count Philip Christopher von Königsmarck has probably been the basis for many romantic love stories; it certainly had all the ingredients.

She was married in 1682 to George Louis, who was son of Sophia, Electress of Hanover, but she fell madly in love with the Count, a dashing handsome Swedish officer and an aristocrat. Unfortunately this love story was to have a very unhappy ending.

Sophia Dorothea's childhood was dominated by her father, the Duke of Celle, perhaps to protect her from the shaky foundation of his marriage to Eleonore d'Olbreuse. Eleonore had refused to lose her virginity to George William unless he married her. This made things tricky for him since he had said he would never marry. In the end George William got his way, and to a certain extent so did Eleonore, because she asked for a contract of marriage, and on 11 November 1665, without any witnesses or church candles, they were technically married.

Later George William, after helping the Emperor Leopold to repel a French invasion, persuaded the Emperor to make Eleonore a Reichsgräfin – Countess of Wilhelmsburg – and in April 1676 George William morganatically married his Eleonore, having been living with her for eleven years.

Sophia Dorothea, their daughter, was to receive from Louis XIV of France a certificate of naturalisation thus giving approval to unsolemnised marriage between George William, her father, and Eleonore, his mistress and her mother.

Sophia Dorothea was engaged to be married to Augustus Frederick of Wolfenbüttel, but he died of wounds at the battle of Philipsburg. The Duke of Wolfenbüttel, the late Augustus Frederick's father, did not want to lose a prime heiress, and his second son was suggested as a husband. However, George Louis – son of Ernest Augustus, Duke of Hanover and Sophia, daughter of the Winter Queen, Elizabeth of Bohemia – was to be her eventual husband.

George Louis had already visited England to woo (Queen) Anne but nothing came of it. Anne thought his manner more in keeping with a barracks than the court, and he could speak no English. Eventually Sophia Dorothea, in 1681 at the age of sixteen, married George Louis and settle in Celle. The marriage was far from easy since he loved battles and military campaigns whereas she was witty and hated the strict protocol of the court at Hanover. They shared the matrimonial bed only occasionally, and after the birth of a son and daughter hardly at all.

Sophia Dorothea was appalled and shocked by her husband's infidelity and argued with him. On one occasion their fighting got so out of hand that he nearly strangled her in his rage. In 1687 various parties and balls were given to celebrate the birth of their daughter and it was at one of these that the handsome officer Count Philip von Königsmarck was introduced to her.

Philip was to inherit his brother's money and title when his brother was killed fighting the Turks. The young count was not immediately attracted to Sophia Dorothea but had eyes on a Charlotte Rantzan, a Danish girl to whom he was on the point of getting engaged; but the affair was broken off and soon afterwards Charlotte Rantzan died. Then there seemed to be a brief association with Countess Platen, a former mistress of the Duke of Hanover. The Count now turned his attentions to Sophia Dorothea. He stepped into the Royal arena very boldly, thinking he could have an affair with the future Duke of Hanover's wife in such a small, close court without being found out.

Count Philip began to write to Sophia Dorothea, and letters, very many letters, arrived via her lady-in-waiting. From the letters it is known that the affair was deepening. The Count wrote from the battlefront: 'I was in agony thinking you have forgotten all about me. I beg of you to give me a chance to see you and say just two words to you and God knows when I shall see you again, my life and my goddess.'

In the early part of 1691 Sophia Dorothea, who until then had conducted her love affair by letter, finally consummated the affair. The flow of letters intensified and the more intimate aspects of their love were discussed. He seemed to be naïve about the risks they were both taking.

He wrote:

I must say that never did a letter arrive more in time, for I was about to accuse you of the blackest treachery; but your letter convinces me that you are incapable of such a thing. It is true that I am not too happy with the cold airs you put on yesterday. That is why I spent such a miserable night. I was so wrought up I could not help crying. I was so agitated my fever returned and I was hot for three hours. Believe me, my divine beauty, that ever since I have known myself, I have never been in such a state. Do you know what I thought? 'God has sent me this illness to punish me, and as if this is not enough, He has also frozen my beloved's heart towards me. This is unbearable, I cannot bear it.' I threw myself down on my knees, my eyes full of tears and begged God, if it were true you did not love me any more to take my life away. I would have welcomed death with all my heart, for I really thought you had turned cold to me.

My pen is not skilled enough to tell you what depth of sorrow I was in, nor can I describe what immense relief your letter gave me. I kissed it a thousand times, and then a thousand more. I hated myself for having thought you capable of inconstancy. I throw myself at your feet and ask your forgiveness, and I promise, and I promise that in future I shall not be so quick to imagine anything like that.

But I beg of you, never be fickle and I do believe that I too am constant. To convince you all the better that I adore no one but you I will sign this with my blood. You must know that as long as you love me you will always be worshipped by

Königsmarck

Signed in blood

And letters like this continued to arrive through 1692 and 1693. The Count was becoming suspicious that the letters were being tampered with, probably by Countess Platen. Perhaps she wanted to use them to turn Ernest Augustus, the Duke of Hanover, against his daughter-in-law. However, he did not seem to be too interested so Sophia Dorothea turned her attention on Count Philip. An impressive military career and popularity with his fellow officers made it difficult for Countess Platen to build up a case against him; she was putting around a rumour that he was planning to buy a more expensive house so he could entertain Sophia Dorothea.

The whole affair had become complicated and at a bad time for Ernest Augustus, Duke of Hanover. He was desirous of becoming the Elector of Hanover, which would mean his name would have to be beyond reproach. The Imperial Edict was made known and Hanover celebrated. The Count wrote:

> Electoral Princess! Now we can call you that, for apparently the Electoral Prince invested you last night with this honourable title. Has his lovemaking more charm now that he has achieved greater rank? I cannot sleep for rage when I think that an Electoral Prince has robbed me of my charming mistress. This morning I would have offered you my congratulations on your new rank, but I doubted whether your husband had done his duty by you. If I am to judge his keenness to see you, the investiture will not start before ten o'clock in the morning.

However all was rather premature: the other powerful German rulers opposed the Duke of Hanover's election.

Count Philip was by now in debt because of his lavish entertaining, and he was drinking heavily. During his drinking bouts he boldly boasted about his love affair with Sophia Dorothea. The plotting and scheming Countess Platen had decided that if Ernest Augustus was not going to act, she would. The Count moved to Herrenhausen and here at the Leine Palace, Sophia Dorothea and Count Philip were to meet for the last time. It is believed they had planned to elope and the Count certainly arrived at the palace before midnight but was never seen again. It is a mystery to this day what happened that night of 1 July. The Countess Platen, assisted by four members of the royal court, almost certainly had Count Philip murdered and the body disposed of.

The Count's papers were seized along with his possessions and Sophia Dorothea knew all was lost. George Louis, her husband, wanted to have her disposed of quickly and the Countess Platen was now in her element. On 17 July Sophia Dorothea was removed from Hanover for the last time and was confined to the Castle of Ahlden, twenty miles from Celle where her father held court.

Now at the young age of twenty-eight in 1695 she took up residence at Ahlden which was to be her place of confinement, her home, her prison for the next thirty-two years.

During those lonely years she was to learn of the death of Countess Platen, who had gone blind and was neglected by the court; of the marriage of her children, the death of William II of England in 1702 and of Queen Anne in 1714, and her husband becoming King of England and being crowned in Westminster Abbey.

Sophia Dorothea, Duchess of Ahlden finally died on 13 November 1726, six months before her husband. She had been Queen of England for twelve years to George I, but she was never to see England and died with just her memories of Count Philip von Königsmarck and a brief love affair that had cost her everything.

Children	Born	Died
George (II)	1683	1760
Sophia Dorothea	1687	1757

George I also had at least two illegitimate children.

George I died 27 May 1723 near Osnabrück and was buried in the chapel of Leine Schloss, Hanover, but his remains were moved after the Second World War to the chapel vaults of Schloss Herrenhausen.

Caroline of Anspach

(Wilhelmina Charlotte Carolina)

Wife of George II

Born 1683

Died 1737

Buried Westminster Abbey

Caroline the Diplomat

George I's son George Augustus was born 10 November 1683 and was George I's only son. When he became George II in 1729 he would rule for thirty-three years.

George Augustus had a strict upbringing. Apart from his princely training he saw service in the army and was the last reigning monarch to lead his army into battle, at Dettingen in 1743.

The heir to the throne should be married, thought the King, and Caroline of Anspach was chosen as his bride. Caroline was daughter of Johann, Margrove of Brandenburg-Anspach, and Eleanor, daughter of the Duke of Saxe-Eisenach. Anspach was part of the Hohenzollern Dominions in the East of Germany. She was regarded as handsome; she was also understanding. As a patron she took great interest in artists, sculptors and musicians. However her first and probably greatest love was politics. She found an ally in Sir Robert Walpole. Walpole had an urge to achieve more and more power. He became the first to hold the title Prime Minister. He ate enormous meals and drank heavily. In one year he spent £1,500 on wines, which today would be excessive. He paid more for the chocolates he ate than the wages of three servants for a year.

George Augustus and Caroline were married in 1705. They were to have three sons and five daughters. The marriage was a happy one, with Caroline showing she could rule the country with the Prime Minister and let the King take a back seat in governmental affairs.

When Caroline was expecting her first child, the Elector (later George I) banned everyone from her apartments except the doctor and midwife – even Caroline's husband and the Elector's wife were told not to enter, and a guard was placed at the door. Eventually the news came that a son had been born, but it was not announced officially until a week later. Was George the Elector being just a little cautious? Did he want to make sure it was a son? And if a son was born dead, was he going to make a switch for a live child of someone else? These questions remain unanswered.

The son was christened Frederick Louis. He was not a particularly healthy child and at one time they thought he had smallpox. His mother Caroline certainly had suffered the disease and this left deep pit marks on her face, which no amount of cosmetics could hide.

It was the year of 1727 that George I died and George Augustus became George II and Caroline became his consort, Although George would rule for thirty-three years, Caroline would be his queen for only ten. Frederick Louis and his father did not get on well together and when Caroline was dying he was refused permission to see her.

Caroline was to die in 1737 and was laid to rest in the Henry VII Chapel of Westminster Abbey. Fourteen years later her son Frederick Louis was to die in 1751. He was born to be king and was hated by the Royal family and by many others but loved by the people. George II died in 1760 and became the last monarch to be buried in Westminster Abbey.

George II had stated that when he died he should be buried with his wife, and they were placed together in a large black marble sarcophagus as if lying in a large double bed.

Children	Born	Died
Frederick	1707	1751
Anne	1709	1759

Amelia	1711	1786
Caroline	1713	1759
Augustus George	1716	stillborn
George William	1717	1718
Miscarriage	1718	
William Augustus	1721	1765
Mary	1723	1772
Louise	1724	1751

Charlotte of Mecklenburg-Strelitz

Wife of George III

Born 1744

Died 1818

Buried St George's Chapel, Windsor

George III was compelled by law to marry a Protestant, and finally, after considering Lady Sarah Lennox he chose Charlotte, younger daughter of Charles Lewis Frederick, Duke of Mecklenburg-Strelitz, and Elizabeth Albertine. Mecklenburg-Strelitz was a small principality in North Germany that few people in England had even heard of.

The betrothal was announced on 8 July 1761. Mr Drummond, the English Ambassador to Prussia, went to Strelitz to perform the betrothal ceremony. The princess was stretched out on a sofa and Mr Drummond then placed his foot on the sofa. This was in part to continue the old practice whereby a girl was put to bed in the presence of her family, while the suitor's ambassador put his leg, which had been stripped to the knee, between the bed sheets as a token of consummation.

Charlotte was duly married to George III on 8 September 1761 and in the space of the following twenty-one years they produced fifteen children and those in turn would produce fifty-six illegitimate children. Three of the children were to die young but most of the others reached old age.

George III was the son of Frederick, Prince of Wales, who never became King because he was killed as the result of being hit by a tennis ball (see the chapter on Augusta, Princess of Wales).

There had been no time wasted in George III marrying Charlotte; the same evening she arrived in the country at 10 a.m. she was married in St James's Palace Chapel Royal, dressed in a silver white gown with a train of velvet trimmed with ermine, with Lady Sarah Lennox at her side as bridesmaid.

Two weeks later George and Charlotte were crowned in Westminster Abbey and by tradition the coronation banquet was held in Westminster Hall. The lavish banquet must have been an overwhelming sight for Charlotte. Having gone through a long coronation ceremony in the Abbey, now she saw hundreds of people in scarlet and velvet gowns, sparkling tiaras and coronets. Like most of these affairs it was well organised but there were one or two mishaps. Someone had forgotten the Sword of State so the Lord Mayor proffered his sword to be used instead. The Lord High Steward, 'Lord for a Day', having entered on horseback and ridden up to the dais to make obeisance, then tried to get the horse to back out of the hall. Despite weeks of training it insisted on travelling along the hall with its rump facing the King and Queen. In Westminster Abbey on the auspicious day the largest jewel in the King's crown fell to the floor. Twenty years later the loss of the American colonies was perhaps the loss of the greatest jewel in the British crown – which some say was foretold in the Abbey that day.

Queen Charlotte was now taking up royal duties. She liked playing cards as a relaxation, though these were banned as being wicked. Princess Augusta, the King's mother, decided that English ladies were forbidden even to approach the Queen without first getting permission from her German attendants. One of the Queen's attendants who had stolen some jewels was sentenced to death, but Charlotte intervened on her behalf and the girl was sent to be a slave on an American plantation.

Charlotte gave birth to the future George IV on 12 August 1762. Her second son was born the following year and he was christened Frederick. This rate of almost a child per year continued for fifteen years. In 1782 the King and Queen's younger son, Alfred, died and the King told the Queen, 'I am sorry for Alfred but had it been Octavius I should have died too!' Only nine months later and just after his fourth birthday Octavius did die. It was in 1783 that the Queen gave birth to her fifteenth child, Princess Amelia.

The King was beginning to suffer from porphyria, which is a

disturbance of the porphyria metabolism, the process that produces pigments which give blood its red colour. This illness can be transmitted from generation to generation. On St George's Day, 23 April 1789, a service was held in St Paul's Cathedral to give thanks for the King's recovery and the King attended the three-hour ceremony.

By 1795 their eldest son, George, was heavily in debt and to clear these it was declared by parliament that George, Prince of Wales should take a wife. The Prince agreed, but took no interest in the choosing of a bride. It was the King who chose the Prince's cousin, Caroline of Brunswick. The Queen quickly realised that Caroline was not the right choice but the couple were married on 8 April 1795 at St James's Palace. Caroline was not the refined sort of woman the Prince might have chosen himself. Her manners and her language left a lot to be desired. Charlotte wanted little to do with the new Princess of Wales. The Queen recruited some of her servants as spies and she became annoyed when she discovered that Caroline referred to the Queen as 'old Snuffy'.

By 1804 the King was suffering again from the old illness and Charlotte now refused to allow the King into her bed. She was becoming fat and ugly and her popularity had disappeared like her figure. The King made his last public appearance on 21 May 1811 and he returned to Windsor on his horse and was not to be seen outside the Castle ever again. He had been King for fifty years and in that time his illness had affected only one year of his reign. Now the King had come to appoint his son Regent. In June 1812 Charlotte visited her husband for the last time, despite the fact he would live for another six years.

The Queen died on 17 November 1818 at Kew, aged seventy-four, and on 29 January 1820, aged almost eighty-two, the King passed away. They left eleven children to survive them but George III had died not knowing about the death of the Queen, or his son the Duke of Kent's death, or the tragic death of his granddaughter Princess Charlotte and her son who died in childbirth.

To the strains of 'I Know that My Redeemer Liveth' the coffin bearing the King was conveyed into St George's Chapel Windsor and so ended a sixty-year reign.

Children	Born	Died
George (IV)	1762	1830
Frederick, Duke of York	1763	1827
William (IV)	1765	1837
Charlotte, Princess Royal	1766	1828
Edward, Duke of Kent	1767	1820
Augusta Sophia	1768	1840
Elizabeth	1770	1840
Ernest, Duke of Cumberland (later King of Hanover)	1771	1851
Augustus, Duke of Sussex	1773	1843
Adolphus, Duke of Cambridge	1774	1850
Mary, Duchess of Gloucester	1776	1857
Sophia	1777	1848
Octavius	1779	1783
Alfred	1780	1782
Amelia	1783	1810
Miscarriage	1764	

George III is said to have married Hannah Lightfoot, daughter of a Wapping shoemaker, who gave him three children.

Caroline of Brunswick

(Caroline Amelia Elizabeth of Brunswick-Wolfenbüttel)
Wife of George IV
Born 1768
Died 1821
Buried in royal vault at Brunswick

Injured Queen of Britain

Prinny, or the Prince of Wales, was married to Mrs Fitzherbert, who herself had had two earlier husbands. He was by 1795 in debt to the tune of £650,000. In order to clear his debts and get Mrs Fitzherbert out of the way it was agreed he would marry his cousin, Caroline of Brunswick. When Caroline arrived in England and he set eyes upon her for the first time, she was worse than he had expected. 'I'm not well,' he said. 'Pray bring me a glass of brandy.' She in turn said, 'I find him very fat and not half as handsome as his portrait.'

On 8 April however they were married. The Prince of Wales was drunk during the brief wedding and had to be supported. When the Archbishop of Canterbury asked whether there was any impediment to lawful marriage the Prince shed tears and the Archbishop had to repeat the question. The honeymoon was spent at Kempshott House, Hampshire, a house which had previously belonged to Mrs Fitzherbert. Lady Jersey, the Prince's mistress accompanied them as lady-in-waiting.

Just nine months later on 7 January 1796 the Prince of Wales announced, 'The Princess, after a terrible hard labour for above twelve hours, is this instant brought to bed of an immense girl, and I assure you, not withstanding we might have wished for a boy, I receive her with all the affection possible.'

The Prince, six months later, felt he had performed his part of the bargain to produce an heir. After his debts were cleared he served formal notice on Princess Caroline of a separation. Feeling free once more, he returned to Mrs Fitzherbert with the blessing of the Pope, who pronounced that Mrs Fitzherbert be the wife of the Prince of Wales according to the law of the Roman Catholic Church.

This peculiar strained relationship between the Prince and Princess made it particularly difficult for the young Princess Charlotte, their daughter. It seemed the Prince wanted a divorce more than anything else so that he could marry again and have sons to deprive Princess Charlotte of the succession. He did say on one occasion that any idea of any child of 'the vilest wretch on earth' sitting on the throne was abhorrent to him.

The Prince of Wales, who all of his life had been far too fat and had too many debts, did not seem to curb his enthusiasms for eating or spending. His extravagances were almost beyond belief. In a fit of spending he bought 100 toothbrushes, shirts by the score, suits by the dozen, thirty-two walking sticks, seven field marshal's uniforms and several hundred whips.

Charles Greville wrote at the time of the Prince's existence:

He leads a most extraordinary life – never gets up till six in the afternoon. They come to him and open the window curtains at six or seven o'clock in the morning; he breakfasts in bed, does whatever business he can be brought to transact in bed took, he reads every newspaper quite through, dozes three or four hours, gets up in time for dinner, and goes to bed between ten and eleven. He sleeps very ill and rings his bell forty times in the night: if he wants to know the hour, though a watch hangs close to him, he will have his valet de chambre down rather than turn his head to look at it. The same thing if he wants a glass of water. He won't stretch out his hand to get it. His valets are nearly destroyed.

However perhaps we should give credit where it is due. The Prince was knowledgeable about art, literature, music and had a comic wit.

In 1806 a tribunal sat at No 10 Downing Street to carry out

what was called the 'Delicate Investigation' and heard witnesses of a supposed adultery by Princess Caroline, the evidence coming from pages, housemaids, footmen, dressers and even friends, all making several statements. Eventually a verdict of 'not proven' was brought in, but society in general, trying to curry favour with the future King George, stopped inviting her to functions and the Prince of Wales refused to attend any function where she might be present. Even Queen Charlotte decided she could no longer receive her at Court.

There were those who sided with the Princess and gave her the affix 'Injured'. Their daughter Charlotte was cared for by some aristocratic ladies, including the Dowager Lady Elgin. The poor little princess had not lived under the same roof as either her father or mother since she had been two years of age. The Prince tried to keep Charlotte from the limelight because he was jealous of her popularity. Lord Grey said in 1813, 'He is jealous of her to a degree of insanity, and has been for some time. While his carriage is met by stony silence or hisses, Charlotte's was saluted by cheers and hurrahs!'

In May of 1816 Princess Charlotte married Prince Leopold of Saxe-Coburg, sealing a new bond which would ensure that future children of the Royal Family would be from the house of Saxe-Coburg. In 1817 Princess Charlotte was expecting a child but unfortunately the boy was stillborn. Shortly afterwards, because of complications of the birth, Charlotte herself was dead. In the course of one night both the heir presumptive and the heir apparent had died, wiping out two generations of the monarchy.

King George III died on 29 January 1820 and the year of 1821 was chosen for the coronation of Prince George, now King George IV, and the date set for 19 July. A quarter of a million pounds was set aside by Parliament for this occasion and George showed just how much of a showman he was by taking the proceedings in hand.

Princess Caroline, now Queen Caroline, asked Lord Liverpool what dress His Majesty would desire her to wear and what ladies of high rank would carry her train. The King had not planned for her to take any part in the ceremony. On the coronation day she drove to the Abbey and tried to gain admittance but was turned away because she had no ticket.

That same year on 30 July, only a short time after the coronation Queen Caroline was seized by abdominal pains while at the Drury Lane theatre. She was taken back to Brandenburg House, Hammersmith and it became clear that the Queen was dying. On the evening of 7 August she passed away. She expressed a wish to be buried in Germany with the inscription on her coffin, 'Caroline of Brunswick, the injured Queen of England'.

Plans were made to convey the Queen's body by sea but the Admiralty had no suitable ship available. Instead a route by road to Harwich was decided upon which was to avoid entering London and the City; but there was a complete mix-up in the arrangements and the coffin made its way down Tottenham Court Road and via Temple Bar and here the Lord Mayor met the coffin and paid his respects on behalf of the City.

She was fifty-three when she died in 1821 and George, who had wanted to be rid of her, probably sighed with relief. Her body was taken to be buried in the Royal Vault at Brunswick. She was laid to rest 26 August 1821.

Children	Born	Died
Charlotte Augusta	1796	1817 (died in childbirth)

George III married Maria Fitzherbert (1756–1837) and she gave him at least two illegitimate children.

Adelaide of Saxe-Meiningen

Wife of William IV

Born 1792

Died 1849

Buried St George's Chapel, Windsor

Princess Adelaide was born at Meiningen, the eldest child of George, Duke of Saxe-Meiningen and Princess Louise Eleanor, daughter of Christian, Prince of Hohenlohe-Langenburg.

She was not considered to be a great beauty, neither did she possess great intelligence, but she did have a kind personality. In 1818, when she was twenty-six, it was arranged that she should marry William, Duke of Clarence, who was twice her age and twice her weight. The marriage proved fruitful even if it did not achieve its purpose and produce an heir, all her pregnancies ended either in miscarriage or in early death.

When Princess Adelaide agreed to marry and came to England, she brought her mother with her and a very small wardrobe of clothes. Adelaide's mother only came because the British government agreed to meet the cost of the travelling expenses.

Lord Reith's daughter, who had previously rejected a proposal of marriage from William, was sent to meet the bride-to-be. When Adelaide and her mother arrived at Grillon's Hotel, Albemarle St, she had a cold reception – there was no one there to meet them. Princess Adelaide was waiting nervously for William to arrive, but it was the Prince of Wales who arrived first to meet his future sister-in-law.

Adelaide had had a good education. She was good at needle-work and she always tried to see the best in everyone, including her future husband, despite his debt and many illegitimate children.

William, who had a naval career from the age of thirteen, had a rather rough form of speech that was frowned on by the society of the day. He liked residing at Bushy, near Hampton Court, although the couple's first residence after their marriage was to be Petersham Lodge.

It was decided the wedding should take place quickly and it was agreed that a double wedding would make a great event. The Duke of Clarence and his brother, the Duke of Kent, would marry their respective princesses, Adelaide and Victoria.

This was indeed a rare affair – the first time a double royal wedding had taken place – but what a strange affair it must have been. The Queen, Charlotte, was ill and not far from death, and if she died suddenly the whole affair would have to be postponed. The Duke of Kent was a field marshal not allowed to go to war, and the Duke of Clarence was an admiral not allowed to go to sea. Neither of the brides could speak English. The brothers who were about to share a church service hated each other, and this religious ceremony was more akin to two horses being put into a starting gate: they were both out to be the first to produce an heir.

Both the brides looked radiant in their wedding gowns – Princess Victoria in gold and Princess Adelaide in silver – for the wedding on Monday, 13 July 1818 at the Palace of Kew. Kew was chosen because Queen Charlotte was too frail to move to any other venue. The Prince Regal gave away both brides.

Just two years after the wedding of these two, George IV died. William, Duke of Clarence, became William IV and Adelaide became his Queen Consort. William had also had a previous love affair with actress Mrs Dorothy Jordan from which there were ten illegitimate children. But William could not produce a legitimate heir. The winners of the marriage stakes on 1818 were therefore the Duke and Duchess of Kent, who produced a daughter, Alexandrina Victoria. William therefore conceded that she would succeed him as monarch.

William's rule was to be but seven brief years and although he attended Victoria's eighteenth birthday in May 1837 he was to die just one month later. When William, died Adelaide became the Queen Dowager and spent the remaining years of her life travelling in England and Europe for the benefit of her health.

She contributed funds to charity on a large scale, including financing the Collegiate Church of St Paul in Valetta, Malta. Adelaide eventually died at Bentley Priory, Stanmore and was buried at St George's Chapel, Windsor in 1849.

Children from Adelaide

Children from Adelaide

Charlotte Augusta	1819	died on the same day
Stillborn	1819	
Elizabeth Georgiana	1820	died 1821
Stillborn	1822	
Stillborn twins	1824	

Children from Mrs Dorothy Jordan (Dorothy Bland)

George Fitzclarence	1794	1842 (committed suicide)
Henry Fitzclarence	1795	1817
Sophia	1796	1837
Mary	1798	1864
Frederick	1799	1854
Elizabeth	1801	1856
Adolphus	1802	1856
Augusta	1803	1865
Augustus	1805	1854
Amelia	1807	1851

Historical Background: Victoria to Elizabeth II

Victoria became Queen at the age of eighteen and was assisted in her early years by Viscount Melbourne, her prime minister. In a sixty-four-year reign there were many changes in industry, education, transport and again further wars abroad. There were wars with China, Afghanistan and the Sikhs; Russian and Crimean Wars; the Indian Mutiny, Franco-Prussian War, Russo-Turkish War, the Zulu War, conflicts in Sudan and Egypt and towards the end of her reign, the Boer War.

On the home front, 1840 saw the arrival of the first postage stamp (the Penny Black). Prince Albert's brainchild of the Great Exhibition occurred in 1884 and was a total success. Albert was to die of typhoid fever ten years later. In the year 1863 came the arrival of the London Underground system, yet it was another five years before the last public hanging took place, in 1868, outside Newgate Prison. Charles Dickens (1812–1870) did much in his writings to bring attention to the plight of the poor and underprivileged.

Victoria died in 1901 aged eighty-two years and was succeeded by her eldest son, Edward. Telegraphy first came into use; the Wright brothers in America flew a plane 852 ft, and within Edward's nine-year reign Blériot would fly the English Channel and aviation was born.

Edward's eldest son, Prince Albert Victor, died before his father, so his second son became King George V. Progress was further advanced by Scott reaching the South Pole in 1912, but he perished with his men on the return journey. The Panama Canal opened in 1913. In 1914 Archduke Franz Ferdinand of Austria and his wife were assassinated at Sarajevo, which led to the outbreak of the First World War, 1914–1918.

George V reigned from 1910–1936. The First World War was to be a very costly affair. It cost Britain and the Commonwealth over £13,000 million and over 1 million men were killed. France lost 1.3 million, Russia 1.7 million, Germany 2 million and Austria 1.7 million.

Women got the vote in 1918 if they were thirty years of age; men had only had to be twenty-one years of age. Sound films came along in 1928.

The King and Queen celebrated their Silver Jubilee in 1935; one year later the King died. He was succeeded by his son Edward, Prince of Wales, as Edward VIII. In the year he became King came the crisis of his wanting to marry Mrs Wallace Simpson, a divorcee. He finally decided to abdicate in 1936 and hand over to his brother, Albert George, who became George VI. Almost as soon as he became King there were rumblings again in Europe and the threat of a further war. This threat materialised in September 1939, when Germany invaded Poland. There followed six years of war. A coalition government under Winston Churchill was formed in 1940. There followed the Blitz, the Battle of Britain, Dunkirk and eventually D-Day, 6 June 1944, an invasion of Europe by Allied forces. The reign of King George VI had been a troublesome period and he died on 6 February 1952 to be succeeded by the present Queen, Elizabeth II.

Victoria

Wife of Prince Albert of Saxe-Coburg-Gotha
Born 1819
Died 1901
Buried Frogmore Mausoleum, Windsor

The Widow of Windsor

The Princess Alexandrina Victoria was born at Kensington Palace on 24 May 1819, the only child of the Duke of Kent, fourth son of George III and Victoria Maria Louisa of Saxe-Coburg, who was the sister of King Leopold of the Belgians. Her father, the Duke of Kent, died when Victoria was eight months old so she was raised by her mother, the Duchess of Kent. It was a strict upbringing by an ambitious and prudish mother. The Duchess did not like William, Duke of Clarence (later William IV), but he did like little Victoria, who would eventually succeed to the throne on William's death.

Victoria was never allowed to do anything on her own; she even had to sleep with her mother until she was sixteen. Victoria's mother made her wear a sprig of holly on the collar of her dress so she would always sit erect at table. A governess was appointed, the Baroness Lehzen, whom Victoria loved and trusted. This strict upbringing, however, was to give her strength of character, and she was a fresh and vivacious young girl. William IV died on 20 June 1837 and young Victoria became Queen at the age of eighteen.

The young Queen's coronation was fixed for 28 June 1838 and the pageantry and pomp of the day lacked nothing. There were one or two mishaps which could have ruined the occasion of the coronation when the Archbishop of Canterbury gave her the heavy orb too soon, the ring was placed on the wrong finger and it took some time to get it off, and, when the peers were paying homage to the new Queen, one peer, eighty-two years old, stumbled and fell twice. The Queen rose from the throne and went to him saying, 'Sir I think I had better come down to you.'

When a husband was being sought for Victoria eyes turned to Saxe-Coburg, since her uncle Leopold had been responsible for some of her early education. Albert, her cousin, was chosen, and they were duly married on 10 February 1840 at the Chapel Royal, St James's Palace. Albert was not to endear himself to the British people; he tended to be tactless, he was certainly serious, and very German. He was eventually to be made a British citizen but was never given the title of an English peer and it was not until 1857 he became by title the Prince Consort.

It has not been disputed that he was a devoted husband and father and in the twenty years of happy marriage there were nine children.

Prince Albert's death in 1861 on 14 December was a devastating blow to Victoria; she had depended on him for so much. Albert left at least two things to remind us of his time in England. One was the Christmas tree, first introduced by him to the royal palace. The second thing was that he planned the idea of the Great Exhibition in 1851, which was a great success, so much so that profit from the proceeds of the exhibition bought the land in Kensington on which now stands the Victoria and Albert Museum, Science Museum, Imperial College of Science and Technology, the Royal College of Music and the Royal Albert Hall.

Victoria now withdrew into the seclusion of her palaces of Balmoral, Windsor and Osborne House on the Isle of Wight. She wore her widow's weeds for the rest of her life and she refused to have Albert's bedroom in Windsor Castle altered in any way. A suit of clothes was laid on his bed and hot water in the bowl was poured daily and fresh flowers strewn on his bed. Even five years after his death she excused herself from opening Parliament because she said she 'did not want to be a spectacle of a poor broken-hearted widow, nervous and shrinking, draped in deep mourning'.

Although she withdrew from public appearances she diligently carried out her royal duties, looking at State papers and signing Acts of Parliament implemented by any one of the ten prime ministers of her reign.

During her reign the British Empire doubled in size. In 1876 she became Empress of India. She was related directly or by marriage to the royal houses of Germany, Russia, Romania, Sweden, Greece, Denmark, Norway and Belgium. She was the first sovereign to travel in a train.

In 1897 at the age of seventy-eight Victoria celebrated her Diamond Jubilee. The whole of the Empire celebrated and Victoria, on a warm summer day, drove to St Paul's Cathedral for a thanksgiving service. As the Queen was old and her eyesight was failing her and she suffered from rheumatism, she sat in her carriage outside St Paul's and the service was held on the steps.

Queen Victoria died on 22 January 1901. Her reign of sixty-four years made her our longest-reigning monarch. She had reigned three years longer and was three days older than George III. It was the end of an era. She was succeeded by her son, Edward VII, and was survived by six children, forty grandchildren and thirty-seven great-grandchildren, including four future kings: Edward VII, George V, Edward VIII and George VI.

She had created Frogmore as the last resting place for her Albert, and she too rests there, away from her Georgian uncles.

Children	Born	Died
Princess Victoria	1840	1901 (Princess Royal) (Married Friedrich III, Emperor of Germany and King of Prussia)
Edward (VII)	1841	1910 (Married Princess Alexandra of Denmark)
Princess Alice	1843	1878 (Married Ludwig IV, Grand Duke of Hesse and by Rhine)

Prince Alfred	1844	1923 (Duke of Saxe-Coburg and Gotha and Duke of Edinburgh) (Married Grand Duchess Maria Alexandrovna of Russia, daughter of the Alexander II, Tsar of Russia)
Princess Helena	1846	1923 (Married Prince Christian of Schleswig-Holstein)
Princess Louise	1848	1939 (Married John Campbell, 9th Duke of Argyll)
Prince Arthur	1850	1942 (Duke of Connaught) (Married Princess Louise of Prussia)
Prince Leopold	1853	1884 (Duke of Albany) (Married Princess Helena of Waldeck and Pyrmont)
Princess Beatrice	1857	1944 (Married Prince Henry of Battenberg)

Alexandra of Denmark

Wife of Edward VII

Born 1844

Died 1925

Buried St George's Chapel, Windsor

The Queen Who Was Always Late

It was the wish of Prince Albert that his son, the future Edward VII, should marry young. In 1858, at the time he was just twenty-one, seven princesses were being considered as his bride. One of these was Alexandra Carolina Marie Charlotte Louise Julia of Schleswig-Holstein-Sonderburg-Glücksberg – a daughter of the Danish Royal House. In September 1861 Edward met Alexandra at the Cathedral of Speyer; he proposed and was accepted. In April 1863 Queen Victoria, accompanied by Prince Edward and Alexandra, went to Frogmore Mausoleum and the Queen declared, 'He gives you his blessing,' meaning Prince Albert, who had died in 1861.

On 10 March 1863 the couple was married at St George's Chapel Windsor, out of the public gaze because the Queen was still in mourning for Albert. She stood behind a curtain and peeped through at the happy couple. The honeymoon was spent at Osborne and the Prince and Princess of Wales then set up house at Marlborough House. There was going to be a long wait for him to become King, almost forty years in fact.

Their first child, a son, was christened Albert Victor and was born 8 January 1864, followed by Prince George (1865), Princess Louise (1867), Princess Victoria (1868) and Princess Maud (1869). There was one other child, Prince Alexander in 1871, but he lived only a few hours. The Princess Louise would eventually marry the Duke of Fife; Princess Maud married Prince Charles of Denmark; Princess Victoria died a spinster and Albert Victor died before his father, so never became King. The second son, George, who married Princess Mary of Teck, would succeed Edward VII.

Albert Victor, the eldest son, seemed to be a problem. He appeared to display weakness of mind, he did not enjoy his time at Cambridge (Trinity College) and a marriage for him was now becoming difficult to arrange. Princess Margaret of Germany, Alix of Hesse and Princess Hélène d'Orléans all came to nothing. Eventually he proposed and was accepted by Princess Mary of Teck but in 1892 Prince Albert Victor, now Duke of Clarence, was taken ill and died of pneumonia.

Queen Victoria passed away on 22 January 1901. The coronation of Edward and Alexandra was arranged for 26 June but had to be postponed.

Lord Torrington, who was regarded as one of the greatest gossips in London, had told of a scandal going around the clubs that Prince Edward was having an affair with an actress, Nellie Clifden, and, as the Victorians would say, had 'lost his purity'. The affair was said to have taken place when the Prince was at camp with the 1st Battalion Grenadier Guards at the Curragh in Ireland. On the Prince's return his father, Prince Albert, went to see him at Cambridge. When Albert returned to Queen Victoria she said he looked tired. He died in December 1861 from typhoid. The Queen came to the conclusion that it was the worry of Edward's conduct that sent Albert to an early grave. After the funeral Prince Edward went on a tour of the Middle East and Jerusalem. On his return he married his beautiful Danish princess and they took themselves off to Osborne where nothing had been touched since Albert's death. It must have been like walking into a morgue for the newlyweds.

The Prince and Princess settled down to married life at Marlborough House. The Princess ignored the Prince's associations with pretty women like Nellie Clifden, Lilly Langtry, Mrs Keppel and the Countess of Warwick.

Princess Alexandra loved her children but admitted that their eldest child, Prince Eddy (as Albert Victor was known within the family), was somewhat slow and shy. She and Prince Edward decided that Eddy should be raised with George, their second son, in the hope that some of the bright and lively interest shown by Prince George would rub off on Eddy.

Prince Eddy was to die young at the age of twenty-eight on 14 December, the same day as Prince Albert. His room was turned into a shrine with a Union Jack draped over his bed, his brush and comb and soap exactly as he left them.

Edward and Alexandra's rule together as King and Queen was to be short, only nine years. By 1906 the King's health began to decline. He suffered an injury to his kneecap on Sir Thomas Lipton's yacht and his other leg he injured tripping over a rabbit hole in Windsor Park – but these were not the main concern, it was the increasing number of bronchial attacks. Finally on 6 May the King collapsed; a series of heart attacks followed and late that night he died.

Alexandra would now step down from her position as Queen and George, her son, and his wife, Mary of Teck, would succeed. Queen Alexandra outlived her husband by fifteen years and died in November 1925 just before her eighty-first birthday.

Children	*Born*	*Died*
Albert Victor	1864	1892 (Duke of Clarence)
George (V)	1865	1936
Louise Victoria	1867	1935 (Princess Royal and Duchess of Fife)
Victoria Alexandra	1868	1935
Maud Charlotte	1869	1938
Alexander John	1871	1871

Mary of Teck

Wife of George V
Born 1867
Died 1953
Buried St George's Chapel, Windsor

Edwardian Queen

> A nation wrapped in mourning
> Shed bitter tears today
> For the noble Duke of Clarence
> And fair young Princess May

The Princess May of Teck, who had been engaged to Prince Eddy, was now mourning his death in 1892. Prince Eddy was in fact Prince Albert Victor, Duke of Clarence and Avondale, eldest son of Edward (VII) and Princess Alexandra. He was nicknamed 'collars and cuffs' as he wore high starched collars because of his long neck.

Princess May of Teck, daughter of the Duke and Duchess of Teck was born at Kensington Palace in 1867. She was very well educated when she met Prince George, who was now heir presumptive to the throne. They fell in love at once. They were engaged in 1893 and married at the Chapel Royal, St James's Palace, on 6 July 1893.

Princess May was actually christened Princess Victoria Mary Augusta Louise Olga Pauline Claudine Agnes, and known to her family as May. Prince Eddy, who was born in 1864, had joined the navy as a cadet but he had been weak from birth and was not to benefit from a life at sea. After meeting May at Balmoral, Eddy proposed during a ball at Luton Hoo and the engagement was announced on 7 December. Queen Victoria was delighted and she had something in common with May since they were both born at Kensington Palace and May's first name was Victoria. The Queen promised them apartments at St James's Palace and the wedding was fixed for February 1892. The Royal Family gathered at Sandringham to celebrate Eddy's twenty-eighth birthday on 8 January but after just two weeks the young prince was dead. What began as a cold developed into influenza, then pneumonia, and he died on 14 January and was buried at Windsor Castle on the 20th.

Prince Eddy's death meant that the second son, Prince George Frederick Ernest Albert, was now heir presumptive at the age of twenty-six. Unlike his brother Eddy, George was stockily built, with blue eyes, sporting a beard and moustache, and he loved the navy. There was now more pressure on him to get married. Eventually George proposed to May on 3 May 1893, the second proposal she had accepted in eighteen months. The wedding was not long delayed and on 6 July 1893 the couple were married at the Chapel Royal, St James's Palace. Presents now began to arrive, reaching a value of £300,000. There were four weddings cakes, one 7 ft in height. The bridal bouquet had the white rose of York predominating, also white orchids, lily of the valley and orange blossom. The wedding dress was white satin with a silver design of roses, shamrocks, thistles and orange flowers and the Princess had three bridesmaids.

So began a comfortable and convenient marriage. Prince George and Princess May had a fondness for each other which was quickly to grow into deep love and devotion and forty-two years of married life.

A two-week honeymoon was spent at York Cottage on the Sandringham Estate, a cottage given to Prince George by his father and always regarded by the Prince as his favourite house. The Prince and Princess were now Duke and Duchess of York and in 1894 their first child, a boy, was born and christened Edward Albert Christian George Andrew Patrick David (the future Prince of Wales, then Edward VIII, who abdicated and became Duke of Windsor). Queen Victoria had expected his first name to be Albert, but Prince George and Princess May pointed out that they wanted Edward as the first name after 'dear Eddy', George's older brother. Queen Victoria was quick to point out that Eddy was not his name, it was in fact Albert Victor. When their second child was born, he was named Albert George (later to be King George VI) and Queen Victoria was asked to be god-mother to the baby prince. The Queen replied 'Most gladly do I accept being godmother to this dear little boy, born on the day his beloved great grandfather entered on an even greater life. He will be especially dear to me.'

Of the other children born to Prince George and Princess May, there were one daughter and three sons. Princess Mary in 1897 (Princess Royal), Prince Henry in 1900 (later duke of Gloucester), Prince George in 1902 (later Duke of Kent) and finally Prince John in 1905. Little Prince John developed epilepsy and finally died aged fourteen in 1919.

With the death of Queen Victoria in 1901 and Edward and Alexandra becoming King Edward VII and Queen Alexandra, Prince George and Princess May's lives began to change. As a future king, George had to be familiarised with affairs of State and from this and his father's trust in discussing politics and diplo-macy with him he gained much that would be of value to him.

They went on an extensive tour of the Commonwealth, visiting Gibraltar, Malta, Aden, Ceylon, Singapore, Australia, New Zealand, Mauritius, Natal, the Cape Canada and Newfoundland. On their return to Britain the King created George Prince of Wales.

A further royal visit took place in 1905, this time to India, an extensive voyage lasting six months. In 1906 they toured Burma. Edward VII's reign was to be fairly short, only nine years; he died in 1910, as Halley's Comet blazed in the night skies.

King George V and Queen Mary, as they now were, were crowned in Westminster Abbey in 1911. A spectacular affair it must have been with representatives from the Commonwealth countries, kings, queens, crown princes from across the world. Lord Kitchener commanded the 50,000 troops lining the route and hundreds of thousands of ordinary people gave the couple a tremendous reception.

Just three weeks after the coronation their eldest son, Edward, was presented as Prince of Wales at Caernarvon Castle.

The King and Queen shared a twenty-six-year reign, including a four-year World War. On 6 May 1935 they celebrated their Silver Jubilee at a thanksgiving service at St Paul's Cathedral, but the King had only seven more months to live. In November 1935 they attended the wedding of their son Henry to Lady Alice Scott, but the King was not able to attend the annual Remembrance Day service at the Cenotaph. On 3 December he was to hear that his sister Victoria had died and the State Opening of Parliament due to be held that afternoon was cancelled – the King was not to appear in public again.

He summoned up the energy and courage to make his Christmas broadcast to the Nation. On the following 20 January the King died. Queen Mary in her diary for that day wrote, 'Am heartbroken at five to twelve my darling husband passed peacefully away.'

The King's body lay in State at Westminster Hall for four days and over 800,000 mourners filed past to pay their last respects to their King. In the funeral procession walked his four sons, five kings, the President of the French Republic and many other leading world figures.

King George and Queen Mary had enjoyed forty-two years of married life and so long ago the pretty girl he had married had grown into a handsome woman and a stately old lady; she never lost her Edwardian image. Her clothes, the famous toques, her parasols, her hairstyle remained until her death. She was tall and walked in a very stately way with erect carriage. After the King's death she took up residence at Marlborough House and over the years watched as her eldest son, Edward, abdicated and her second son became King George VI until his death in 1952. She saw her granddaughter Elizabeth become Elizabeth II, but she would not live to see her coronation. She may well have had a premonition that her life was coming to an end. She told the Queen that should she die before the coronation date of 3 June 1953, the coronation should proceed as planned.

Queen Mary passed away on 24 March 1953 and the coronation did proceed as planned. She was eighty-five years of age.

With the death of Queen Mary ended the last vestiges of the

Edwardian era. Despite the fast-moving pace of the twentieth century she was able to hold on to her own way of life, her own pace of life and to all she always looked every inch a Queen.

Children	*Born*	*Died*
Edward (VIII)	1894	1972 (Married Mrs Wallis Simpson; became Duke of Windsor)
George (VI)	1895	1952 (Married Lady Elizabeth Bowes-Lyon)
Mary (Princess Royal)	1897	1965 (Married 6th Earl of Harewood)
Henry	1900	1974 (Duke of Gloucester) (Married Alice Montagu-Douglas-Scott, daughter of 7th Duke of Buccleuch)
George	1902	1942 (Duke of Kent) (Married Princess Marina of Greece and Denmark; killed in plane crash)
John	1905	1915 (died as a result of an epileptic fit)

Lady Elizabeth Bowes-Lyon

Wife of George VI

Born 1900

Died 2002

Buried St George's Chapel, Windsor

Prince Albert George, Duke of York, first met the Lady Elizabeth Bowes-Lyon in 1920 at a small private dance. They met again in 1921. She was the ninth child of the Earl and Countess of Strathmore, a very old Scottish family. She was a scintillating dancer and full of sparkle. They eventually became engaged in 1922 and the wedding was planned for Westminster Abbey in April 1923. 'Bertie [the Prince's family nickname] was supremely happy,' wrote Queen Mary.

During the wedding ceremony in Westminster Abbey there was a delay in the proceedings when one of the clergy fainted. While Lady Elizabeth waited for the procession to reform she suddenly left the Prince's side and placed her bouquet of white York roses on the tomb of the Unknown Soldier in memory of her brother who was killed in the First World War.

After their honeymoon in Scotland they took up residence in White Lodge, Richmond Park. The house proved too large and too expensive to run and the Duchess wanted something in central London. Eventually they found what they wanted. After a brief stay at Chesterfield House they moved into 145 Piccadilly. It was however at 17 Bruton Street on 21 April 1926 that their first child was born and she was christened Elizabeth Alexandra May. 'Elizabeth of York sounds so nice,' wrote the King. A second daughter was born in August 1930 and christened Margaret Rose. She was born at Glamis Castle in Scotland.

King George V and Queen Mary celebrated their Silver Jubilee in 1935 but the King was to die a few months later in 1936.

On 20 January 1936 the Prince of Wales became King Edward VIII but as yet not married. Edward seemed to be in every way the king of a monarchy of the modern age. It was not long however before the matter of the King's association with Mrs Wallis Simpson reared its ugly head. She was invited to Balmoral Castle in the autumn, much to Queen Mary's displeasure and this was the feeling possibly of all the Royal Family. Edward had not yet expressed that he wished to marry Mrs Simpson. During the summer and autumn things were changing; the government threatened to resign but Mr Baldwin the Prime Minister refused to put that sort of ultimatum to the King. Mrs Simpson's decree nisi became absolute on the grounds of collusion. Edward finally met Mr Baldwin and said he meant to go through with the marriage. 'I have looked at it from all angles and I mean to abdicate and marry Mrs Simpson.'

There were attempts to make him change his mind. Queen Mary argued with him but he refused to budge. Most of the Commonwealth countries were against a marriage with Mrs Simpson. On the weekend of 5–6 December 1936 he decided finally he would abdicate. The instrument of abdication was signed and he left for France.

For the Duke of York and his Duchess this was a testing time. It was a harsh and unwelcome way to begin a reign. Prince Albert George, Duke of York, now became King George VI and his wife Elizabeth became his Queen Consort. When talking to his cousin Lord Louis Mountbatten, the King said, 'I never wanted this to happen, I'm quite unprepared for it. David has been trained for this all his life. I've never seen a State paper. I'm only a naval officer, it's the only thing I know about.'

Queen Elizabeth was of immense support to the new King. The coronation took place on 24 May 1939.

The King and Queen were only just getting into their role when war broke out. The two princesses were sent out of London but the King and Queen remained giving moral support to the people and they too suffered the ravages of war when Buckingham Palace was bombed.

After more than five years of war the King had the task of leading his people into a new era. They were naturally delighted to be reunited with the princesses since the King and Queen were worried that they had missed a vital part of their growing up.

In 1947 it was announced that the Princess Elizabeth would marry Lieutenant Philip Mountbatten and he was created His Royal Highness the Duke of Edinburgh. Their first child, Charles Philip Arthur George, was born in November 1948 much to the delight of the King and Queen.

During March 1949 the King underwent surgery; the strains of war, the strains of their South African tour and the stresses and strains of monarchy were taking their toll. There was a possibility he may have had to have his right leg amputated but the operation was successful. Eventually cancer was diagnosed and the King underwent a further operation in September 1951. The following 30 January 1952, he went to the airport to bid farewell to Princess Elizabeth and Prince Philip on their way for a tour of Australia. In Kenya on a stopover Princess Elizabeth was told that her father had died and that she was now Queen as of 6 February 1952.

Queen Elizabeth now became the Queen Mother and moved from Buckingham Palace to Clarence House. In the ensuing fifty years she tirelessly carried out royal engagements until the end of her life. She was by far the most popular member of the Royal Family during her lifetime. She gave immense service to the country and her beauty and charm and her motherly ways touched many hearts and set the tone for the Royal Family in a changing world.

She became the first lady to hold the position of Lord Warden of the Cinque Ports and all of the positions she held she carried out with interest, with diligence and with perfection.

She died in 2002 aged 101 and is buried at Windsor with her husband. King George VI.

Children	Born	Died
Elizabeth (II)	1926	
Margaret Rose	1930	2002 (Countess of Snowden) (Married Antony Armstrong-Jones 1960, divorced 1978)

Elizabeth II

Wife of Prince Philip Mountbatten
Born 1926

Queen Elizabeth II

Elizabeth Alexandra May, daughter of King George VI and Queen Elizabeth, was born on 21 April 1926 at 17 Bruton Street, Mayfair, home of the Earl and Countess of Strathmore. It was thought that she might have been christened with Victoria in her name, something that Queen Victoria had intimated for future heirs. When George V heard that her names would not include Victoria he said it didn't really matter as she was not likely to be queen.

After the abdication of Edward VIII, when his brother became King George VI, it automatically made Princess Elizabeth the heir presumptive.

In 1947 it was announced that the princess would marry Prince Philip Mountbatten, a Royal Navy officer. Prince Philip was born in Corfu on 10 June 1921. He was the fifth child and only son of Princess Alice, a great-granddaughter of Queen Victoria, and Prince Andrew of Greece. The Greek family were exiled to England between 1923 and 1935, when Prince Philip was educated at Cheam, Gordonstoun and the Royal Naval College at Dartmouth. He served in the navy in the Second World War. He became a British subject in 1947 and adopted the name Mountbatten. This was the anglicised form of his mother's family of Battenberg. Just before he married Princess Elizabeth he was created Duke of Edinburgh by King George VI.

The Princess Elizabeth and Prince Philip were married in Westminster Abbey on 20 November 1947.

The Princess left for a tour of Australia with Prince Philip in 1952 and they stopped in Kenya en route. While up a tree in a safari park in the Treetops Hotel she was told the news that her father the King had died on 6 February 1952. Immediately the Princess became a Queen and they both returned to London.

Just over a year later on 2 June 1953 the coronation took place in Westminster Abbey. HM Queen Elizabeth was crowned by the Archbishop of Canterbury, continuing an almost unbroken tradition that has taken place for over 900 years. There were two exceptions: Edward V, who was the young prince murdered in the Tower of London in 1488; and Edward VIII, who abdicated and became Duke of Windsor.

And so began the reign of the second Queen Elizabeth.

On the day of the coronation it was announced that Mount Everest had been climbed by Sir Edmund Hillary and Sherpa Tenzing. That same year Joseph Stalin died. The following year, 1954, on 3 July food rationing ended after fourteen-and-a-half years. Prince Charles was created Prince of Wales in 1958. Sir Winston Churchill died on 24 January 1965. In 1969 Prince Charles had his investiture as Prince of Wales at Caernarvon Castle. This same year Neil Armstrong became the first man to set foot on the moon. Decimal currency was introduced on 15 February 1971 and Britain joined the European Economic Community on 1 January 1973.

We have during this present reign celebrated royal weddings. Princess Margaret, Princess Anne, Prince Charles and Diana Spencer, Prince Andrew and Sarah Ferguson. The Queen has celebrated her silver wedding, her Silver and Golden Jubilees and her 80th birthday.

I feel that the majority of Her Majesty's people would agree that we have been more than fortunate to have a monarch who has carried out all her duties – be they everyday activities, overseas tours, of which there have been many, investitures, processions, Trooping the Colour and much more – without an obvious hitch. There must be the occasional hiccup in such a meticulous way of life. If so, we the public don't see it. For more than fifty years she has been our Queen and we hope she will carry on for many more years.

God bless the Queen!

Children *Born*

Charles	14 November 1948 (Prince of Wales) (Married Lady Diana Spencer (1961–1997); divorced 1996; married Camilla Parker Bowles 2005)
Anne	15 August 1950 (Princess Royal) (Married Mark Phillips; divorced 1992; married Timothy Laurence 1992)
Andrew	19 February 1960 (Duke of York) (Married Sarah Ferguson; divorced 1996)
Edward	10 March 1964 (Earl of Wessex) (Married Sophie Rhys-Jones)

Queen Elizabeth II has (to date) eight grandchildren: Prince William of Wales, Prince Henry of Wales, Peter Phillips, Zara Phillips, Princess Beatrice of York, Princess Eugenie of York, Lady Louise Windsor and James, Viscount Severn.

Some key events

Charles, Prince of Wales and Lady Diana Spencer married in 1981

Charles and Diana divorced in 1996

Diana, Princess of Wales, killed in car crash, Paris 1997

Princess Margaret died aged 71 in February 2002

Queen Elizabeth, the Queen Mother, died aged 101 in March 2002

Charles, Prince of Wales married Camilla Parker Bowles in 2005

The Princesses of Wales

It was Edward I who created his son, another Edward, as the first Prince of Wales. Twenty more Princes of Wales were to follow but there have only been eight Princesses of Wales, five of whom went on to become Queen. Those five have already been discussed. The three Princesses who did not become Queen – Joan of Kent, Princess Augusta and Lady Diana Spencer – are the subjects of the following section.

1. Joan of Kent – married Edward the Black Prince

2. Catherine of Aragon – married Prince Arthur then Prince Henry (Henry VIII)

3. Caroline of Anspach – married George II

4. Princess Augusta – married Frederick, Prince of Wales

5. Caroline of Brunswick – married George (later George IV)

6. Alexandra of Denmark – married Edward (later Edward VII)

7. Mary of Teck – married George (later George V)

8. Lady Diana Spencer – married Charles, Prince of Wales

Joan of Kent, Princess of Wales

Wife of Edward, the Black Prince

Born 1328

Died 1385

Buried Stamford

The Fair Maid of Kent

Edward of Woodstock, later known as the Black Prince, was born at Woodstock on 15 June 1330. He was the eldest son of Edward III and Queen Philippa of Hainault. He inherited from his father his warlike qualities and a love for pomp and tournaments.

During the fourteenth century the Hundred Years War broke out between England and France. The war began in 1338. The Black Prince first fought in 1346, aged sixteen. He fought nobly at Crécy and Poitiers. Although the origin of the title 'Black Prince' is not certain it may well refer to the colour of his armour or to the colour of the livery worn by his retainers.

Edward the Black Prince was made a Knight of the Garter, a founder knight of the twenty-six in 1348.

When Edward wanted to find a wife he chose Joan, Countess of Kent, who had been married twice previously. Her first husband was Sir Thomas Holland but she was also married to the Earl of Salisbury in Sir Thomas's absence. Sir Thomas Holland was furious and had the marriage to the Earl dissolved, conveniently for Joan as Sir Thomas died leaving her a desirable widow. After complicated negotiations with the Pope the way was made clear for Edward to marry Joan.

Joan was one of the most beautiful women of her age and justly deserved the title 'Fair Maid of Kent'. As a thanks offering to the Pope for allowing the marriage Edward founded a chantry chapel in the crypt of Canterbury Cathedral with two altars to the Holy Trinity and to St Mary the Virgin. Their marriage was a happy one. In 1362 the Prince was made Duke of Aquitaine and Gascony and then he went to Bordeaux where he and Joan kept a very sumptuous court. It was while at Bordeaux that their son Richard was born in 1367. He would later become Richard II.

There broke out more trouble with Charles V of France. Because of the extravagances at the Prince's court the French King asked him to come to Paris to answer for his misgovernment and taxation of the people to pay for these expensive displays, tournaments and banquets. The Prince said he would gladly go to Paris 'but it would be with a helmet on my head and sixty thousand men in my company'. He eventually besieged Limoges in 1371 and put many of the citizens to the sword.

Two years after Limoges, the Black Prince returned to England. The Prince was now ill. Years of battle campaigning had taken their toll and on Trinity Sunday, 8 June 1376, he died. It was the day 'all through his life he had kept holy'.

In his will he asked that his bequests be made and his debts paid, and that Joan should have a third of his estate. Almost his last words to those gathered around his bed concerned his son: 'I commend to you my son, who is very young and little and pray you, as you have served me, to serve him loyally.'

Also in his will he asked to be buried in Canterbury Cathedral in the Chapel of Our Lady in the Undercroft. This request was disregarded as it was deemed more fitting he should be buried in the Trinity Chapel near the shrine of Thomas Becket.

Joan, the Princess of Wales, retired to the Manor of Kennington. She had been the first Princess of Wales and her marriage to Edward, the Black Prince, seems to have been one of the few sincere love matches of the arranged marriages of those so young.

When she died in 1385, nine years after her husband, she was buried at Friars Minor in Stamford.

Children	Born	Died
Richard (II)	1367	1400

Augusta, Princess of Wales

Wife of Frederick Louis, Prince of Wales

Born 1719

Died 1772

Buried Westminster Abbey

When George II's son Frederick Louis, Prince of Wales was looking for a wife, or more to the point when his father was, thoughts naturally turned to the royal families in Germany, and one name that came to the forefront was the little principality of Saxe-Gotha.

Augusta was just seventeen years of age and not the most beautiful of princesses. Her first meeting with her new family did not start well – she was an hour late and George II was always so punctual. Frederick Louis and Augusta, however, seemed to get on well with each other. The bad start she had with George II was soon overcome by the new Princess of Wales when she showed she had character and intelligence.

In 1737 the Princess Augusta was pregnant with her first child. They had been married on 27 April 1736. The whole Royal Family had gone to Hampton Court Palace but Frederick and Augusta, who went along by order of the King, found the whole idea very depressing. On 31 July Frederick and Augusta attended morning service and the arrival of their child seemed to be the last thing on anyone's mind. In the Prince and Princess of Wales' apartments, soon after they retired, the first signs of labour started. Frederick decided then and there that his child should not be born under the same roof as his father and he ordered a coach to be taken to London and St James's Palace, despite protests from the Princess and the ladies-in-waiting. Although his wife was in agonising pain the Prince still insisted they travel. It was almost

10 p.m. when the coach arrived at the Palace, which was in total darkness – the Princess was quickly bedded down between tablecloths, since no sheets could be found. The official witnesses were called and soon the new prince was born.

When the King and Queen found out that Frederick and Augusta were back at St James's Palace, they were, to say the least, extremely annoyed. The King issued instructions that they should both be banished from the palace; they were to take no furniture and the court officials were instructed to have nothing to do with them. Frederick and Augusta did not seem to be particularly put out by the banishment; in fact they seemed to relish the thought. They took up residence at Kew and also used Norfolk House and Carlton House.

Frederick did not see his parents for seven years, as they left him in Germany when George ascended the throne and came to England. He was not invited to his father's coronation. However, when Frederick arrived in the country he was popular with the English people. It is a strange trait of the Georgian kings that the father often hates the son. George I hated his son George (later George II) and now George II was showing his hatred for Frederick. They perhaps saw their eldest son as a threat to the throne, particularly if they became popular at court and with the people.

Frederick Louis may have had a premonition of his early death at the age of forty-four. He spent time putting his papers in order and wrote a long letter to his son, the future George III, of how he should conduct himself when he became King. Frederick, Prince of Wales attended a tennis match and was hit on the head by a tennis ball. There were complications that developed into pneumonia from which he died.

The funeral was a very quiet affair with members of the royal family conspicuously absent. The Jacobites did not care for the Hanoverians, and a witty verse of the day stated the following:

> Here lies poor Fred
> Who was alive and now is dead.
> Had it been his father
> I had much rather.

Had it been his brother
Still better another.
Had it been his sister
No one would have missed her.
Had it been the whole generation
Still better for the nation.
But since 'tis only Fred
Who was alive and is dead
There's no more to be said.

An interesting point was that before Frederick married Princess Augusta he was offered the hand of the youngest granddaughter of the Duke and Duchess of Marlborough, namely Lady Diana Spencer, but Robert Walpole, the Prime Minister, intervened by saying the Prince had already been promised to Augusta.

Children	Born	Died
Augusta	1937	1813
George (III)	1738	1820
Edward	1739	1767 (Duke of York)
Elizabeth Caroline	1740	1759
Henry	1745	1790 (Duke of Cumberland)
Louisa Anne	1749	1768
Frederick William	1750	1765
Caroline Matilda	1751	1775

Diana, Princess of Wales

Wife of Charles, Prince of Wales

Born 1961

Died 1997

Buried Althorp Estate

The People's Princess

Prince Charles Philip Arthur George was born 14 November 1948 at Buckingham Palace. It had been fifty-five years since the birth of the last boy who had become Prince of Wales. Charles went to prep school at Cheam on the Berkshire Downs then to Gordonstoun, his father's old school. Charles also had a period at Geelong School in Australia, and he also went to Cambridge. He eventually joined the Royal Navy and spent a term at Aberystwyth University learning Welsh. He became Prince of Wales in 1958 but it was not until 1969 that he was invested with the title.

On 28 February 1981 the announcement was made that Lady Diana Spencer would marry Prince Charles. The wedding took place at St Paul's Cathedral on 29 July 1981. An estimated 600,000 people lined the route from Buckingham Palace to St Paul's. The marriage produced two sons, William Arthur Philip Louis and Henry Charles Albert David, commonly known as Prince Harry.

Diana became 'The People's Princess' as a loving mother and one involved with the work of various charities.

You could tell she had a love of children and she raised two wonderful sons – not just to be Royal princes, but also to meet with and enjoy the company of other children. Her charity work was varied and extremely worthwhile.

When she died in 1997 after a car crash in Paris, the outpouring of grief and hundreds of flowers laid at the gates of the palaces at Kensington and Buckingham were a testament to how much she was loved by the nation and would be missed.

Children	*Born*
William of Wales	21 June 1982
Henry of Wales (Harry)	15 September 1984

Tables

SOVEREIGNS SINCE THE CONQUEST
QUEENS REGNANT
QUEENS CONSORT
PRINCESSES OF WALES
PRINCESSES ROYAL

Sovereigns Since the Conquest

N	Norman
P	Plantagenet
L	Lancaster
Y	York
T	Tudor
S	Stuart
H	Hanover
W	Windsor

	King/Queen	Ruled	Reign
N	William I	21 years	1066–1087
N	William II	13 years	1087–1100
N	Henry I	35 years	1100–1135
N	Stephen	19 years	1135–1154
P	Henry II	35 years	1154–1189
P	Richard I	10 years	1189–1199
P	John	17 years	1199–1216
P	Henry III	56 years	1216–1272
P	Edward I	35 years	1272–1307
P	Edward II	20 years	1307–1327
P	Edward III	50 years	1327–1377
P	Richard II	22 years	1377–1399
L	Henry IV	14 years	1399–1413
L	Henry V	9 years	1413–1422
L	Henry VI	39 years	1422–1461
Y	Edward IV	22 years	1461–1483

	King/Queen	Ruled	Reign
Y	Edward V	2 months	1483
Y	Richard III	2 years	1483–1485
T	Henry VII	24 years	1485–1509
T	Henry VIII	38 years	1509–1547
T	Edward VI	6 years	1547–1553
T	Mary I	5 years	1553–1558
T	Elizabeth I	45 years	1558–1603
S	James I	22 years	1603–1625
S	Charles I	24 years	1625–1649
	Interregnum	11 years	1649–1660
S	Charles II	25 years	1660–1685
S	James II	3 years	1685–1688
S	William and Mary	13 years	M 1689–1694
			W 1689–1702
S	Anne	12 years	1702–1714
H	George I	13 years	1714–1727
H	George II	33 years	1727–1760
H	George III	60 years	1760–1820
H	George IV	10 years	1820–1830
H	William IV	7 years	1830–1837
H	Victoria	64 years	1837–1901
H	Edward VII	9 years	1901–1910
W	George V	26 years	1910–1936
W	Edward VIII	11 months	1936
W	George VI	16 years	1936–1952
W	Elizabeth II		1952–

Queens Regnant

1. Mary I, reigned 1553–1558
2. Elizabeth I, 1558–1603
3. Mary II, 1689–1694
4. Anne, 1702–1714
5. Victoria, 1837–1901
6. Elizabeth II, 1952–

Queens Consort

1. Matilda of Flanders, wife of William the Conqueror
2. Matilda of Scotland, wife of Henry I
3. Adela of Louvain, Henry I
4. Matilda of Boulogne, Stephen
5. Eleanor of Aquitaine, Henry II
6. Berengaria of Navarre, Richard I
7. Avisa of Gloucester, John
8. Isabella of Angoulême, John
9. Eleanor of Provence, Henry III
10. Eleanor of Castile, Edward I
11. Margaret of France, Edward I
12. Isabella of France, Edward II
13. Philippa of Hainault, Edward III
14. Anne of Bohemia, Richard II
15. Isabella of France, Richard II
16. Mary Bohun, Henry IV
17. Joan of Navarre, Henry IV
18. Catherine de Valois, Henry V
19. Margaret of Anjou, Henry VI
20. Elizabeth Woodville, Edward IV
21. Anne Neville, Richard III
22. Elizabeth of York, Henry VII
23. Catherine of Aragon, Henry VIII

24. Anne Boleyn, Henry VIII

25. Jane Seymour, Henry VIII

26. Anne of Cleves, Henry VIII

27. Catherine Howard, Henry VIII

28. Katherine Parr, Henry VIII

29. Anne of Denmark, James I

30. Henrietta Maria, Charles I

31. Catherine of Braganza, Charles II

32. Anne Hyde, James II

33. Mary of Modena, James II

34. Sophia Dorothea of Celle, George I

35. Caroline of Anspach, George II

36. Charlotte of Mecklenburg-Strelitz, George III

37. Caroline of Brunswick, George IV

38. Adelaide of Saxe-Meiningen, William IV

39. Alexandra of Denmark, Edward VII

40. Mary of Teck, George V

41. Lady Elizabeth Bowes-Lyon, George VI

Princesses of Wales

1. Joan of Kent, wife of Edward, The Black Prince
2. Catherine of Aragon, wife of Henry VIII
3. Caroline of Anspach, George II
4. Princess Augusta, Frederick, Prince of Wales
5. Caroline of Brunswick, George IV
6. Alexandra of Denmark, Edward VII
7. Mary of Teck, George V
8. Lady Diana Spencer, Charles, Prince of Wales

Princesses Royal

1. Mary, daughter of Charles I and Henrietta Maria
2. Anne, daughter of George II and Caroline
3. Charlotte, daughter of George III and Charlotte
4. Victoria, daughter of Queen Victoria and Prince Albert
5. Louise, daughter of Edward III and Alexandra
6. Mary, daughter of George V and Queen Mary
7. Anne, daughter of Queen Elizabeth II and Prince Philip

Printed in Great Britain
by Amazon.co.uk, Ltd.,
Marston Gate.